OPPOSING
VIEWPOINTS®
SERIES

The Aging Population

Other Books of Related Interest:

Opposing Viewpoints Series
Health Care

Current Controversies
The Elderly

At Issue Series
Seniors and Driving

"Congress shall make
no law . . . abridging
the freedom of speech,
or of the press."

First Amendment to the U.S. Constitution

The basic foundation of our democracy is the First Amendment guarantee of freedom of expression. The *Opposing Viewpoints* Series is dedicated to the concept of this basic freedom and the idea that it is more important to practice it than to enshrine it.

OPPOSING VIEWPOINTS® SERIES

The Aging Population

Katherine Swarts, Book Editor

GREENHAVEN PRESS
A part of Gale, Cengage Learning

GALE
CENGAGE Learning™

Detroit • New York • San Francisco • New Haven, Conn • Waterville, Maine • London

Christine Nasso, *Publisher*
Elizabeth Des Chenes, *Managing Editor*

© 2009 Greenhaven Press, a part of Gale, Cengage Learning

Gale and Greenhaven Press are registered trademarks used herein under license.

For more information, contact:
Greenhaven Press
27500 Drake Rd.
Farmington Hills, MI 48331-3535
Or you can visit our Internet site at gale.cengage.com

For product information and technology assistance, contact us at

Gale Customer Support, 1-800-877-4253
For permission to use material from this text or product, submit all requests online at www.cengage.com/permissions

Further permissions questions can be emailed to permissionrequest@cengage.com

Articles in Greenhaven Press anthologies are often edited for length to meet page requirements. In addition, original titles of these works are changed to clearly present the main thesis and to explicitly indicate the author's opinion. Every effort is made to ensure that Greenhaven Press accurately reflects the original intent of the authors. Every effort has been made to trace the owners of copyrighted material.

Cover image copyright iofoto, 2008. Used under license from Shutterstock.com.

LIBRARY OF CONGRESS CATALOGING-IN-PUBLICATION DATA

The aging population / Katherine Swarts, book editor.
  p. cm. -- (Opposing viewpoints)
Includes bibliographical references and index.
ISBN 978-0-7377-4236-7 (hardcover)
ISBN 978-0-7377-4237-4 (pbk.)
1. Aging--Juvenile literature. 2. Older people--Juvenile literature. I. Swarts, Katherine.
  HQ1061.A4297 2009
  305.260973--dc22

                                                            2008033998

Printed in the United States of America
1 2 3 4 5 6 7 12 11 10 09 08

Contents

Chapter 3: What Social Implications Does an Aging Population Present?

Chapter 4: What Is the Role of Science in the Aging Process?

Why Consider
Opposing Viewpoints?

> *"The only way in which a human being can make some approach to knowing the whole of a subject is by hearing what can be said about it by persons of every variety of opinion and studying all modes in which it can be looked at by every character of mind. No wise man ever acquired his wisdom in any mode but this."*
>
> John Stuart Mill

In our media-intensive culture it is not difficult to find differing opinions. Thousands of newspapers and magazines and dozens of radio and television talk shows resound with differing points of view. The difficulty lies in deciding which opinion to agree with and which "experts" seem the most credible. The more inundated we become with differing opinions and claims, the more essential it is to hone critical reading and thinking skills to evaluate these ideas. *Opposing Viewpoints* books address this problem directly by presenting stimulating debates that can be used to enhance and teach these skills. The varied opinions contained in each book examine many different aspects of a single issue. While examining these conveniently edited opposing views, readers can develop critical thinking skills such as the ability to compare and contrast authors' credibility, facts, argumentation styles, use of persuasive techniques, and other stylistic tools. In short, the *Opposing Viewpoints* series is an ideal way to attain the higher-level thinking and reading skills so essential in a culture of diverse and contradictory opinions.

In addition to providing a tool for critical thinking, *Opposing Viewpoints* books challenge readers to question their own strongly held opinions and assumptions. Most people form their opinions on the basis of upbringing, peer pressure, and personal, cultural, or professional bias. By reading carefully balanced opposing views, readers must directly confront new ideas as well as the opinions of those with whom they disagree. This is not to simplistically argue that everyone who reads opposing views will—or should—change his or her opinion. Instead, the series enhances readers' understanding of their own views by encouraging confrontation with opposing ideas. Careful examination of others' views can lead to the readers' understanding of the logical inconsistencies in their own opinions, perspective on why they hold an opinion, and the consideration of the possibility that their opinion requires further evaluation.

Evaluating Other Opinions

To ensure that this type of examination occurs, *Opposing Viewpoints* books present all types of opinions. Prominent spokespeople on different sides of each issue as well as well-known professionals from many disciplines challenge the reader. An additional goal of the series is to provide a forum for other, less known, or even unpopular viewpoints. The opinion of an ordinary person who has had to make the decision to cut off life support from a terminally ill relative, for example, may be just as valuable and provide just as much insight as a medical ethicist's professional opinion. The editors have two additional purposes in including these less known views. One, the editors encourage readers to respect others' opinions—even when not enhanced by professional credibility. It is only by reading or listening to and objectively evaluating others' ideas that one can determine whether they are worthy of consideration. Two, the inclusion of such viewpoints encourages the important critical thinking skill of objectively evaluating an author's credentials and bias. This evaluation will illuminate an author's reasons for taking a particular stance on an issue and will aid in readers' evaluation of the author's ideas.

It is our hope that these books will give readers a deeper understanding of the issues debated and an appreciation of the complexity of even seemingly simple issues when good and honest people disagree. This awareness is particularly important in a democratic society such as ours in which people enter into public debate to determine the common good. Those with whom one disagrees should not be regarded as enemies but rather as people whose views deserve careful examination and may shed light on one's own.

Thomas Jefferson once said that "difference of opinion leads to inquiry, and inquiry to truth." Jefferson, a broadly educated man, argued that "if a nation expects to be ignorant and free . . . it expects what never was and never will be." As individuals and as a nation, it is imperative that we consider the opinions of others and examine them with skill and discernment. The *Opposing Viewpoints* series is intended to help readers achieve this goal.

David L. Bender and Bruno Leone,
Founders

Introduction

"Life expectancy nearly doubled in the 20th century. Since 1900, the number of Americans age 65 and older has increased 10-fold. . . . In 1950, only about 3,000 Americans were centenarians; by 2050, there could be nearly one million."
—Doug Dollemore, Office of Communications and Public Liaison, National Institute on Aging, U.S. National Institutes of Health

As recently as the 1930s, the average human life span was under the official retirement age of sixty-five. A male U.S. citizen who celebrated his twenty-first birthday in 1896 had slightly less than a 54 percent chance of making it to his sixty-fifth birthday; a woman, slightly better than 60 percent. Every decade since has added three to six points to those percentages; and, with the corresponding decrease in childhood mortality, overall life expectancy has climbed from sixty-three to seventy-six years. Even before the enormous baby boom population—those born between 1946 and 1964—has reached age sixty-five, there are already ten times as many Americans over that age as in 1900. Today's seniors are more independent and vigorous on average than were their early-twentieth-century counterparts, too. If Social Security benefits were adjusted to reflect these changes, few people today would be eligible to collect before age seventy or eighty.

There also has been a corresponding increase in the age at which people perceive themselves as old. The once-common quip that "no woman wants to admit to being over thirty" is rarely heard anymore, certainly not as often as "seventy [or eighty] is the new fifty." "[Business news network] CNBC is dominated by frisky septuagenarians," wrote *Newsweek* columnist Daniel Gross in June 2008. "Advances in medicine make the retirement age of 65 seem like a relic. . . . CT Partners, the executive search firm, recently conducted an unscientific poll on its Web site, asking managers whether they'd hire a 72-year-old CEO [chief executive officer]. . . . The answer was yes, by a margin of 55–45 percent."

Experts believe that the centenarian population will multiply by fifteen in the twenty-first century. Medical advances mean fewer people die from once-deadly diseases. (Cancer in the 1930s was fatal far more often than not; today, about half of cancer patients recover, and with early treatment some survival rates are as high as 95 percent.) Moreover, the health conscious can now find in mere seconds on the Internet lists of tips for the best chances at achieving long, healthy lives through diet and exercise. A one-week tracking survey by the Pew Charitable Trusts, in November 2004, reported that 79 percent of Internet users—95 million American adults—performed some health-related online research during that time and that thirty to sixty-four was the most common age range for doing so.

The same proactive attitude prevails in most other aspects of life. Fewer people now plan to spend their retirement years gardening, reports journalist Victoria Knight in a 2007 *Wall Street Journal* article:

> Past generations of Americans viewed a leisurely retirement as a reward for years of hard work. For trend-setting baby boomers who rocked the world, the prospect of whiling away the hours—actually more likely two decades—in a rocking chair can inspire dread rather than delight. A Gallup Poll in June of 2006 found that one-third of working adults are very or somewhat concerned about "losing a sense of purpose" in their lives after they retire. . . .
>
> "People that report the highest degree of satisfaction in retirement are those who are actively engaged," said Maureen

Mohyde, director of Corporate Gerontology at The Hartford Financial Services Group Inc. Part-time work, community groups, charities, studying or even a second career can provide such outlets, she said.

Even before retirement, a take-charge attitude is evident in Americans during the working years. Rather than staying for an entire working lifetime at the same company, the average American now changes jobs ten times—and careers three or four times—between the end of education and the end of salaried income, reports the U.S. Department of Labor. Americans these days choose their careers less according to family tradition and potential income and more according to personal fulfillment, too. Perhaps this change will eventually lead to a reduction in the retirement rate itself, as more people will remain employed because they enjoy their jobs as well as because they need the income.

As for those who do retire from paid employment, large numbers are volunteering their time. "For years, volunteers over age 50 represented just 1 percent of the Peace Corps' ranks," reported *Newsday* in February 2005. "But in recent years, the number of 50-plus volunteers has jumped to 6 percent of the total." And Eldertreks, "the world's first adventure travel company designed exclusively for people fifty and over," has been in business since 1987.

Still, as people over sixty-five encompass a majority of the population and people over eighty-five become commonplace, a correspondingly increasing worry is that they will eventually put too much strain on society's resources. *Opposing Viewpoints: The Aging Population* looks at varying conclusions on four related issues: What Are the Prevailing Attitudes Regarding the Aging Population? How Should Government and Business Help Support the Aging Population? What Social Implications Does an Aging Population Present? and What Is the Role of Science in the Aging Process?

OPPOSING
VIEWPOINTS®
SERIES

CHAPTER 1

What Are the Prevailing Attitudes Regarding the Aging Population?

Chapter Preface

In many nontechnological societies, to be called "old" has traditionally been considered a compliment. Besides placing value on the wisdom and experience of long life, these societies often have short individual life expectancies so that seventy- or eighty-year-olds are unique and respected.

Contrast this to the attitude of modern Western society, where such pejorative phrases for the elderly as "worn out," "senile," "useless," or at best, a condescending "sweet" predominate. Perhaps it is because the United States itself is relatively young among world societies or perhaps because it has built its reputation on innovation, but Americans generally have taken the attitude that once people pass their sixty-fifth birthdays, they are no longer valuable contributors to society.

Now, however, there is emerging a trend toward acceptance regarding the elderly as the nation grows older by leaps and bounds and as individuals live longer. In fact, the oldest members of the largest demographic age group of the population—the baby boomers, born from the mid-1940s to the mid-1960s—has passed the age sixty mark at a time when those in their seventies and eighties are increasingly defying the stereotype of being worn out and aged. Consider readers' reactions to the historical novel *Though None Go with Me.* Author Jerry B. Jenkins set his story in the early years of the twentieth century, when people rarely lived beyond age fifty, and followed his protagonist over several decades of an overall hard life. His commitment to accuracy regarding her aging was not universally applauded: "I was criticized by several readers (particularly elderly women) for making my main character fairly decrepit by age sixty-five. . . . Today, sixty-five is considered late middle age, and we expect to remain active into our eighties."

Despite the aging of society and the youthfulness of many older Americans, some commentators point out that there still seems to be a stigma associated with growing old and looking old. Professional speaker Mariah Burton Nelson states, "Most African-Americans do not appreciate hearing, 'You don't look black. Yet we still praise each other [by saying]: 'You don't look your age.' . . . As long as we insinuate with our language that there's something wrong with being old, people will continue to discriminate against the obviously old."

The increasing ways available to fight the signs of the onset of aging, such as Botox injections, plastic surgery, and fat implantations, may be indicators of society's resistance toward aging.

Are Americans moving toward acceptance of old age, or are they fighting it at every opportunity? Does old age always go hand in hand with an onset of dementia? This chapter explores these and other related topics.

> *"Middle-ageism teaches us to blame aging for the loss of hope and the crushing of dreams, instead of putting the blame where it should lie."*

Society Is Prejudiced Against Aging

Margaret Morganroth Gullette

In the following viewpoint, Margaret Morganroth Gullette argues that society's prejudice against the middle-aged hurts not only the victims of such stereotypes, but ultimately the whole population. Pressure to retire as early as fifty-five is becoming common, and could lead to increased stress for older workers, depression among victims of "early exit," and general demoralization of the entire country, she says. Gullette is a resident scholar at the Women's Studies Research Center of Brandeis University in Waltham, Massachusetts, and the author of Declining to Decline: Cultural Combat and the Politics of Midlife *and* Safe at Last in the Middle Years.

As you read, consider the following questions:

1. What percentage of French workers between ages fifty-five and sixty-four does Gullette report have been "pushed out" of the workforce?

2. According to Gullette, on what wrong issue does journalist Susan Sheehan's *New Yorker* article on a fifty-one-year-old victim of downsizing focus?

3. What change that might benefit middle-aged employees has France made in its workweek?

When there's a Viagra to be marketed, "midlife diseases" like male sexual dysfunction are "discovered," there is rising horror at normal wrinkles; anti-aging "necessities" like preventive facelifts are recommended earlier.

Without seniority, legal or customary, many people aging into midlife internalize their worthlessness. In the working class people say they feel "old" younger than those in the middle class do—and they don't mean they feel more mature. ("You're only as old as you feel," the saying goes. But "how old" you feel and how young you begin to "feel" old may be a function of gender, class, or other prejudice—of lack of seniority in conjunction with debilitating labor, lack of access to medical care, and other avoidable sources of distress.) To add insult to injury, mainstream writers are now chanting the delights of "retiring" at fifty-five. Sure, on what pension?

Middle-Aged Retirement in France

To guess our own future if we do nothing, we could start by critically looking abroad. The news we are permitted to hear from France about age in relation to the workforce describes people cheerfully looking forward to retiring to pleasant second homes at fifty-five. The facts are quite different, as anyone who watches the movies of Laurent Cantet (*Human Resources*, *Time Out*) already guesses. A full half of French workers between fifty-five and sixty-four have been pushed out of the workforce. Even "50 to 54-year-olds are now caught up in this trend; their employment rate fell by seven percentage points from 1975 to 1988," writes Anne-Marie Guillemard, whose essays are extraordinary in including so much detail about the psychological consequences and about social indifference to their plight. In this harsh new world, even having employment at midlife carries with it permanent anxiety about losing one's job, with any renegotiations occurring from the employee's situation of reduced power. The "preretired" (horrible term, echoing "preseniors") are treated as one with the prematurely superannuated. One way or the other, the social value of the entire group from fifty to sixty-four in public opinion polls is sinking toward zero. Although the young are also seriously unemployed, Guillemard writes, "This is the only age group to which this has happened. The others' positions have oscillated between 13 and 11 on this 20-point scale."

No Clear Understanding of Midlife Condition

Here in the United States, after unemployment insurance runs out, there is no safety net until Social Security kicks in, perhaps years later. How a needy group fares morally and economically and even legally (as *Kimel* [*Kimel et al. v. Florida Board of Regents* (2000), in which the U.S. Supreme Court ruled that states might use age as an employment criterion] shows) depends on how it is represented—it depends on "needs interpretation," and that in turn depends on the "character" the group is given. Given the media's lack of coverage— not to mention its misrepresentations of the Boomers [those Americans born in the post–World War II era known as the baby boom]—the public has no clear picture of midlife conditions over recent decades. If we fail to prevent and reverse the trends, we will have the leisure to contemplate whether it's worse for midlifers to be invisible or demonized. One tactic that serves the free market's ruthlessness is having the commerce in aging involve us in interminable inner debate about whether at midlife people are "too old" (to be useful workers) or "too young" (to be inactive). People at midlife could be both too old and too young—fixed in a tragic "natural" bind—so sad, but nothing to do. Except defy "aging."

Media Condescension Toward the Middle-Aged

Even before they are perceived as a group, an ideological contest to represent the prematurely superannuated is shaping up, with the left trying to show them as primarily diverse, hardworking for decades, able, and unwilling to go quietly into the jobless future, and the rest portraying them as losers. [*Pulitzer Prize–winning journalist*] Susan Sheehan wrote in the *New Yorker* about a family in which the fifty-one-year-old father had lost a good job. "I know I'll never be able to earn $11.80 an hour again," Kenny Merten recognized. "The most I can hope for is a seven-dollar-an-hour job that doesn't involve swinging sandbags." Although Merten was partly disabled, a victim of a downsizing economy, lacking education and a union, Sheehan discussed the couple's financial imprudence at length, bringing in a consultant to help them with poverty management. (In a confessional mode that [sociologist Michel] Foucault and Richard Sennett have explained, they had given her their detailed financial records.) Condescension could well be the lot of any of us with drooping age/wage curves.

The discursive side of middle-ageism is useful to a system opposed to seniority and trying to prevent the anger of the superannuated. Middle-ageism imputes losses of ability (slower reflexes, techno-retardation) so that layoffs and downgrading of "deadwood" have some show of justification. In an era where computers have phenomenal "memory," memory loss is incorrectly represented as a problem peculiar to the midlife. Middle-ageism takes advantage of the cult of youth. The defects of the middle years are contrasted explicitly with the entrepreneurial, physical, sexual, intellectual, and creative accomplishments of the young. Anti-middle-ageist forces are put on the defensive, trying to argue through *proofs* why

"How Dare You Assume That I'd Rather Be Young!"

I abhor being addressed as "Young lady." I'm not in denial about my age so why should anyone else be? Sometimes it might be a nasty form of sarcasm, but I doubt it. It's usually in some ignorant, misguided way, based on the unfortunate premise in our society that everyone would rather be young. Therefore, it's meant to flatter. When an admirer commented to Maggie Kuhn, founder of the Gray Panthers, that she looked young for a woman in her seventies, her response was, "How dare you assume that I'd rather be young!"

Eugenie G. Wheeler, The Time of Your Life:
The Best of Genie Wheeler's Columns on Aging Issues, *2005.*

midlife workers are superior. Instead of admiring their adult children for doing well, some parents are humiliated or bitterly envy their age class. Middle-ageism teaches us to blame *aging* for the loss of hope and the crushing of dreams, instead of putting the blame where it should lie: on the mechanisms of postindustrial global capital.

Changing What It Means to Be Human

Shortsightedly driving wages down, the agents of these changes are also blind or indifferent to their effects. They are not only losing the abilities of midlife individuals and damaging their lives. By tinkering with the life course at the midlife, in the long run they are also changing what it means to be human.

The French example shows how this comes about. Decades of dealing with "early exit" are marked by inadequate planning, demonstrating in part the lack of ethical theorizing about the place of the midlife in the life course. Companies continue as much as they legally can to cut midlife employees from the workforce at the lowest possible cost, and the public authorities refuse as far as politically possible to take responsibility for the formerly employed. Even the patchwork responses are shredded as soon as they begin to cost too much (read: work too well). Programs called "unemployment" and "disability" have been the preferred means of interpreting need, but when it appears that too many "older" workers utilize them, they are reread as "welfare."

Age Discrimination in Employment Becomes Normalized

Worst of all, once the "logic" of substituting the labor of a younger age group for that of an older has come into play, it is hard to put an end to it. The practice can become explicitly normalized, as when midlife workers are praised for giving up jobs "for their children." France has given dramatic proof of solidarity with labor by imposing a thirty-five-hour week; this might help midlifers. But Guillemard believes that an improvement in the French labor market will not lead back to the situation prior to the early-exit trend. The devaluation of the age class becomes a part of social understandings of the life course, an institutionalization of the work span that seems "natural." Only those who remember an earlier system know in their hearts that this apparently natural succession is false, but their sense of history has been a priori nullified. In an economy saturated with decline, the happy few who benefit from seniority cannot by themselves reinstate it. I know many middle-class educated people in our own country who are aware that their security is fragile. Some are hoping to weather the national midlife crisis without ignominy and exit voluntarily by their own timing, leaving decline behind for the rest.

Potential Midlife Crisis for the Nation

Once decline has been administered at midlife, we never regain powers that we are unable to exercise. Disempowered, embittered, some people withdraw from action, hedge the generosity of their politics—not so mysteriously turning into the conservative midlife caricatures we were taught to deride and anticipate. If aging were the problem, how could anyone resist *that*? A population clinging to a decline view in a period of fabulous fortunes and painful inequality may not see the contradictions. Many are blinded by the ideology that economic chances are private and natural; they may become yet more self-involved, atomized, and subdued. A nation demoralized in such ways is dangerous—likely to be mean-spirited to "losers" domestically; and, distracted by paranoia, hostile and belligerent abroad. In such ways the devaluation of the midlife constitutes a collective "midlife crisis" for the nation. This is the nightmare we should be trying to avert.

> "Even if society has a long way to go be-
> fore we overcome negative stereotypes,
> the images that active [seniors] . . .
> project already are changing younger
> people's ideas about aging."

Society Is Becoming More Accepting of Aging

David Oliver Relin

While the word "old" still tends to evoke negative images, people in the age range once called old are increasingly defying those stereotypes. As a result, reports journalist David Oliver Relin in the following article, seniors now have a long list of suggested new labels for the over-fifty population, including "seasoned citizens," "the Re-Generation," and "Legacy Launchers." Even the younger population, noticing its elders' new images, is changing its attitude toward aging. Relin, whose writing and editing have won over forty national awards, is a contributing editor for PARADE Magazine.

As you read, consider the following questions:

1. What segment of the over-sixty population does Relin report is having the most genuine difficulties?

2. What word does one seventy-four-year-old cited in the viewpoint hate to hear added to a description of seniors' activities?

3. What new name for the sixty- to eighty-year-old generation does one seventeen-year-old suggest in the following viewpoint?

This year [2006], the first wave of Baby Boomers [people born in post–World War II America] turns 60. Now that so many people are living longer with good health and vitality, traditional phrases like "senior citizen" and "elderly" seem outdated. "Clearly, the old language of aging no longer reflects people's active lives," says Susan Moses of the Harvard School of Public Health. *PARADE* [magazine], along with the Harvard School of Public Health and the MetLife Foundation, asked readers for names that better describe this stage of life. Nearly 4,000 responses poured in.

"Senior Citizens?" no thanks, said Cynthia Solaka of Charlotte, N.C. She has a different thought: "seasoned citizens."

"Seasoned because the varying experiences of a lifetime— both sweet and sour—make us what we are," wrote Solaka, 52. "Aging allows you to separate the important from the unimportant, to appreciate more and reach for less, to allow those younger to step up to the plate and learn their lessons."

Dozens of readers warned us not to paint too rosy a picture of life after 60. And, in general, those with medical or financial problems found this stage of life challenging. "Many of us are one mortgage payment away from being homeless or a broken hip away from a county home," wrote Savannah Blaze Lee of Quilcene, Wash., who will turn 60 next year [2007]. "I would call us 'The Forgotten,'" she said.

The vast majority, however, had nothing but good news to report from the far side of 60. Many readers said that they find themselves in the prime years of their lives. In fact, one of the most popular terms suggested for the 20-year span between 60 and 80 was "prime time."

"As a 73-year-old Chinese-American, I am reveling in what I call the 'Age of Dignity,'" said Parkman Joe of Berkeley, Calif., who divides his time between ballroom dancing with his wife of 40 years and sharpening his speaking skills at his local Toastmasters Club. "In Chinese culture, we venerate the elderly," Joe said. "I'm hard at work teaching my fellow American septuagenarians to revel in their age of dignity."

LeAnne Reaves, 57, of Hurst, Tex., said she and her friends have happily begun the journey toward the 60-to-80 age group. "A few of us have crossed kicking and screaming," Reaves reported. "But most of us simply have awe, wonder and appreciation for the fact that we actually have made it to this level of life. I think the name that characterizes us is 'OWLS,' for Older, Wiser, Livelier Souls."

For some, it is a wealth of new opportunities and activities that defines this stage of life. Readers suggested terms like "Life 102," "The Third Half," "Geri-Actives" and the "Re-Generation." And there were stories about skydiving, studying new languages, traveling to the ends of the earth and finding pleasure in mastering new skills that once were considered too time-consuming when life was centered around the demands of earning a living and raising children.

"In the past few years, I've mastered things I wanted to do all my life—like gardening and horse training," revealed Margot Doohan, 60, of Bozeman, Mont. "It's my practice to present an image that encourages younger females to say, 'That's what I want to be when I grow up.'"

Many were infuriated by the media's attitude toward older Americans in a youth-dominated culture. "I'm 74, and I ski, swim and stand on my head in yoga," said De Vee Lange of San Diego. "And I'm frustrated by society's attitude of putting the word 'still' in front of these activities."

The Advantages of Renting to Older Tenants

Senior citizens make great tenants, said Karen Kopas, a longtime community manager for Walker House, a small rental high-rise in Montgomery Village, Gaithersburg [Maryland], where about 40 percent of the building's tenants are older than 60. "They're quiet; they're clean; they take care of the building. They pay the rent on time, by the way," she said. "We love to have them."

On a basic level, low residential turnover saves in painting and cleaning costs for a new tenant. Longtime residents also are more likely to care about a building, Kopas said. Young people usually are more transient, while seniors often stay for years.

Karen Tanner Allen, Washington Post, *August 23, 2003.*

But even if society has a long way to go before we overcome negative stereotypes, the images that active people like Doohan and Lange project already are changing younger people's ideas about aging. "Folks in their 60s to 80s seem almost a brand-new generation," wrote Rachel Powell, 17, of Rochester Hills, Mich. "They are participating in activities I would never even dream of them doing and are reinventing how older people live. I suggest calling them the 'Re-Invented Generation.'"

Several readers sent us similar terms for what they describe as a period of passionate renewal. "Because there are so many productive, energetic Baby Boomers ready to forge into their second stage, I would rename this period 'Rewirement,'" said Virginia Monaghan, 59, of Monessen, Pa., a retired teacher who now writes children's books and volunteers for local charities.

Indeed, a committed army of readers marched to their mailboxes to tell us that giving back to society is what makes this stage rewarding. They proposed names like the "Givebackers," "Longivety" and "Legacy Launchers." "Give" is the key word, said Joan Larsen, 73, of Park Forest, Ill. Larsen added that "we should not only call this the 'Giving Stage' but also make it happen. When you give, the years drop away, you beam, and your heart is full to bursting. Isn't that what life is all about?"

That, and keeping a sense of humor about life's twists and turns. Many readers, like Alan Brown, 66, of Plantation, Fla., wrote to tell us that maintaining a light-hearted attitude is the secret to happiness. "I'd call life after 60 the 'Metallic Stage,'" Brown said. "It is so named for the silver in your hair, the gold in your teeth, the tin ear you're developing, the platinum credit card you're being offered, the titanium implant in your hip and the lead in your behind."

"Denial of aging seems to be the rule in our society, not the exception."

People Are Afraid of Growing Old

Andrew Weil

In the following selection, Andrew Weil looks at—and denounces—the aging-denial phenomenon of which he sees many manifestations in contemporary America: heavy use of cosmetics and cosmetic surgery; revulsion at the sight of outwardly aged people; and physical injuries suffered by those who push themselves into activities better suited to younger bodies. Dr. Weil, a leading proponent of natural health and wellness, is founder and director of the Arizona Center for Integrative Medicine (a department of the University of Arizona). His books include Spontaneous Healing, Eight Weeks to Optimum Health, *and* Healthy Aging, *from which this viewpoint was taken.*

As you read, consider the following questions:

1. According to Weil, before what age do many women undergo their first cosmetic surgeries?

2. What is one reason Weil gives to explain why many young people have an aversion to older people?

3. Besides cosmetic surgery, what is one common way in which middle-aged women attempt to deny aging, according to the viewpoint?

It is fine to use [cosmetics] if you enjoy them, if they make you feel good, if you are using them to make yourself more beautiful and more attractive to your own eyes and to the eyes of others. I would ask you, however, to look carefully at your motivations and make sure they do not include a desire to undo the normal changes in appearance that aging brings. If that desire is present, you are vulnerable to the unfounded claims of manufacturers who want to take your money and to seduction by the fantasy that you can stop, slow, or reverse aging. That path leads away from acceptance of a natural and universal process central to our experience as human beings. Following it will make it harder for you to master the art of healthy aging.

Obviously, cosmetic surgery can be an even more powerful and costly seduction, not to mention a riskier one. Once available only to the most affluent, it has recently become much cheaper, much more mainstream, and much more widely practiced. More than 70 percent of those who opt for cosmetic surgery today earn less than $50,000 a year.

As with cosmetics, people resort to surgery to alter their appearance for very different reasons. When they do it to repair birth defects like harelips or damage from trauma, I have no quarrel with it. (That is properly called reconstructive rather than cosmetic surgery.) When young people get nose jobs or breast augmentations, I may consider their actions frivolous, but it is not of great concern to me unless the procedures pose significant risks to health. But when I see increasing numbers of older men and women getting face-lifts, Botox injections, and fat implantations to fill in wrinkles, I do worry.

We have all seen disastrous results of plastic surgery: procedures that did not heal or, more commonly, faces pulled so tight that their owners look like the Bride of Frankenstein. And these less appealing outcomes of surgical alteration of the face become more grotesque as people age. Of course, the procedures can be done skillfully and can give more pleasing results. So if cosmetic surgery makes people feel better about themselves, makes them feel more beautiful and attractive, and therefore gives them better quality of life and improves their relationships, again, it is probably not my place to argue against it. But I think it is a problem when their primary reason for having plastic surgery is to pretend that aging is not occurring.

Remember that your true age—your biological age—is determined not by years but by the state of your body's structure and functions. That probably has to do with the balance between oxidative stress and antioxidant defenses, with the accumulation of errors in the DNA of your cells, with the extent of caramelization that has occurred in your tissues, with the integrity of your mitochondria. In the words of a female plastic surgeon, "It happens one day. You're fine until a certain point because you can't see what happens inside your body, and then one day you see signs of aging in your face. It's a sharp reminder of mortality." Plastic surgery cannot fix what happens inside your body; it can only dull the sharpness of the reminder. And, to my mind, that is movement away from reality. I agree with [early-twentieth-century psychiatrist] Carl Jung, who wrote: "As a physician I am convinced that it is hygienic . . . to discover in death a goal toward which one can strive; and that shrinking away from it is something unhealthy and abnormal which robs the second half of life of its purpose." *Because aging reminds us of our mortality, it can be a primary stimulus to spiritual awakening and growth.*

The relative percentage of men seeking cosmetic surgery has not changed in the past twenty years, while that of women

Postponing Aging with Hair Coloring

There's a reason why forty, fifty, and sixty don't look the way they used to, and it's not because of feminism, or better living through exercise. It's because of hair dye. In the 1950s only 7 percent of American women dyed their hair; today there are parts of Manhattan and Los Angeles where there are no gray-haired women at all. . . .

Hair dye has changed everything, but it almost never gets the credit. It's the most powerful weapon older women have against the youth culture, and because it actually succeeds at stopping the clock (at least where your hair color is concerned), it makes women open to far more drastic procedures (like face-lifts). I can make a case that it's at least partly responsible for the number of women entering (and managing to stay in) the job market in middle and late middle age, as well as for all sorts of fashion trends. For example, it's one of the reasons women don't wear hats anymore, and it's entirely the reason that everyone I know has a closet full of black clothes. Think about it. Fifty years ago, women of a certain age almost never wore black. Black was for widows, specifically for Italian war widows, and even Gloria Steinem might concede that the average Italian war widow made you believe that sixty was the new seventy-five. If you have gray hair, black makes you look not just older but sadder. But black looks great on older women with dark hair—so great, in fact, that even younger women with dark hair now wear black.

Nora Ephron, I Feel Bad About My Neck: And Other Thoughts on Being a Woman, *2006.*

has skyrocketed. And women are undergoing it at ever-younger ages, often getting their eyes done before they reach forty.

"How is it really," asks essayist Daphne Merkin, writing about the subject as her fiftieth birthday approaches, "that American women have been so successfully terrorized by the thought of showing their age—of becoming what even the fiercely independent-minded lesbian writer May Sarton described as 'an old woman, a grotesque miserable animal'—that they will spend enormous amounts of money and time in the effort to stave off a process that was once considered to be a natural, even revered one by any means, ranging from the patently ludicrous to the purportedly scientific to the bloodily effective?" She also includes this comment from a medical researcher at Columbia University [in New York]: "Aging is nature's way of preparing us for death. That's why we hate old people."

I was surprised to hear that kind of hatred coming from a friend of mine, a woman only slightly younger than I [in her sixties], who teaches yoga, does grief counseling, is well read in the literature of many spiritual traditions, and is not afraid to talk about death and dying. I think of her as a wise elder or, at least, a person in the process of becoming one.

"I never admitted to myself how repelled I am by old people," she told me recently. "I was walking on the beach and saw an old couple coming toward me, maybe in their mideighties. They had their arms around each other, and I know I should have applauded the fact that they were out walking together and being affectionate, but all I could see was the sagging flesh, those wattles under the chin, and I had to look away. Then I had to face the degree of my antipathy toward them. I hate people who look that way. Their appearance repels me, especially their faces. This was a revelation for me, not a comfortable one."

I can find no explanation for her reaction other than the obvious one. She sees in these people what she will become, and she hates them for reminding her of it. . . .

I see so many middle-aged men who have injured themselves because they did not stop running or playing basketball long after they should have stopped and found other forms of physical activity. I see so many middle-aged women who resort to cosmetic surgery or maintain relentless social and work schedules to keep up with younger women. As I said, denial of aging seems to be the rule in our society, not the exception.

You might wonder how much of it I do. There is nothing like writing a book on aging to force you to confront it in yourself. I do not use antiaging cosmetics and have no interest whatever in cosmetic surgery. I still engage in activities, including some higher-risk ones that might be more appropriate for younger men. (I chased severe storms for a few weeks of the past two summers and got a bit too close to a tornado that tore up the little town of Happy, Texas, on May 5, 2002. This past summer I ran with the bulls during the festival of San Fermin in Pamplona, Spain.) But I assess risks carefully and so far have not come to harm, even if I may have given my guardian angels a lot of work. On the other hand, I have been able to let go of many activities as I have moved away from my youth. In my thirties and forties, I did a great deal of backpacking in wilderness areas. Today, if I consider such trips, I think how nice it would be to have a pack animal rather than carrying all that camping gear on my shoulders.

I like my face as it is and am not in the least tempted to color my beard black, as it was long ago. In fact, looking at my white beard in the mirror gives me good opportunities to reflect on the positive aspects of aging, on the real rewards it can bring.

> *"Trying to turn back the clock is passé as a quiet revolution emphasizes that well-being is the key to quality of life and peace of mind."*

People Are Becoming Less Afraid of Growing Old

Stacie Stukin

The following viewpoint looks at the changes that are taking place in the aging population's attitudes toward their health practices and lifestyles, emphasizing that desperate attempts to cling to youth are losing momentum and that more middle-aged and older people are focusing on healthy everyday activities that are enjoyable but not radical. Today's most popular lifestyles, Stacie Stukin reports, include meditation and other spiritual/religious practices, diets specific to individual needs, and building exercise opportunities into daily routines. Stukin is a freelance journalist in West Hollywood, California, who writes frequently on health-related topics.

As you read, consider the following questions:

1. According to Stukin, what types of cosmetic surgery procedures are becoming increasingly popular?

2. How many hours of meditation per week have researchers found improve decision-making and sensory-processing skills, according to Stukin?

3. As cited by the author, how much daily exercise is recommended?

A funny thing happened on the road to perfection. Suddenly, enjoying your exercise routine is more important than going for the burn. Meditation is edging out the shrink's couch. And trying to turn back the clock is passé as a quiet revolution emphasizes that well-being is the key to quality of life and peace of mind.

"I like to call it 'pro-aging' or 'successful aging,'" says Miriam Nelson, an associate professor at the Friedman School of Nutrition Science and Policy at Tufts University in Boston. "There are still those who panic about getting older and get depressed with each passing year. Then there is another, growing group of people who are thinking about what they can do to be as vigorous as possible to reduce their incidence of age-related disease by eating well, exercising, managing stress and being happy and connected."

Adapting to Aging

"It's a move to adapt to aging, to value it and honor what it means to grow old in this era of unprecedented longevity," says Fernando Torres-Gill, director of the Center for Policy Research on Aging at UCLA [University of California at Los Angeles]. "People are . . . taking responsibility for their health without relying on quick fixes like pills or surgery."

Integrative medicine proponents such as Andrew Weil have built businesses on books and beauty and health products. Medi-wellness spas, such as David Murdock's California WellBeing Institute at the Four Seasons Hotel in Westlake Village, offer the best in medicine with alternative approaches to prevention.

The following primer outlines some of the freshest approaches to looking and feeling your best now . . . for a generation of Americans who are embracing every stage of life as "prime time."

Cosmetic Surgery "To Improve What's Already There"

With all this talk of pro-aging, it's hard to avoid the subject of cosmetic surgery. Although it's a popular option for many, some simply don't want a nip and tuck. According to the American Society of Plastic Surgeons, the number of face-lifts declined 4% between 2005 and 2006. Beverly Hills plastic surgeons such as John Vartanian are noticing a shift. Vartanian says about 25% of his patients just want to improve what's already there. "There's a subpopulation who are maturing and who grew up with the option of cosmetic surgery," he says. "But they don't want an extreme look; they want to look natural." Part of this is due to new options in the surgeon's toolbox. In particular, nearly 9 million Americans opted for minimally invasive procedures in 2006. Those scalpel-free procedures leave no scars and require no downtime or hiding. People are resurfacing their skin with lasers, filling in fine lines and wrinkles with injectable material and using Botox to prevent lines and crevices. "I love those patients," says Vartanian. "They have common sense, they don't want to look freaky and I can make them happy."

Religion and Health

After the terrorist attacks of Sept. 11 [2001], the *New England Journal of Medicine* reported that 90% of Americans turned to religion to cope with the stress. Although that finding echoes many national surveys about the prevalence of religious participation among Americans, particularly those 65 and older, the medical scientific community is just beginning to understand how personal religious belief systems affect well-being and health. "In the last 10 years it's become more and more evident that there is a positive relationship between religion and health," says Harold G. Koenig, a professor of psychiatry and behavioral sciences at Duke University who has authored some of that research. Koenig says religious people are happier, more hopeful, recover more easily from illness and adapt better to changes that come with aging or challenging situations. Because religion, or any spiritual pursuit, promotes a positive attitude toward aging, there's evidence that that attitude will, in fact, help you live longer.

The Popularity and Benefits of Meditation

The National Centers for Complementary and Alternative Medicine estimates that more than 15 million Americans meditate regularly. "The best way to accept the stage of life you find yourself in is to do some self-investigation," says Susan Smalley, a professor of psychiatry at the Semel Institute at UCLA. "That's when you gain understanding, wisdom and ultimately happiness." Film director David Lynch does it. So does [former U.S. vice president] Al Gore. Top-tier hospitals use it, as do Fortune 500 companies. It's done in locker rooms and even in prisons. "Meditation helps your mind be healthier," says Victoria Maizes, executive director of the University of Arizona's Program in Integrative Medicine. "That, in turn, helps your body respond better to challenges." Reams of scientific data prove it can help with chronic pain, arthritis, asthma, PMS [premenstrual syndrome], depression and other conditions. In 2005, a study at Massachusetts General Hospital in Boston demonstrated that the brains of people who meditated six hours a week on average had thicker gray matter in the area responsible for decision-making, attention and sensory processing. Another recent study suggested that brain waves of meditators are more active in the area associated with happiness and optimism.

Aging Can Bring a New Freedom

I have been blessed to know many men and women who, when they reach the age of fifty or sixty, begin to free themselves from cultural constraints and to express themselves in ways they had not dared to do before. They become less defined by what others think of them and more by what they think of themselves. Increasingly freed from the burden of having always to fulfill other people's expectations, their lives start to reflect a new kind of willingness to be exactly who they are. . . .

Instead of thinking of it as a tragedy when their bodies begin to creak and slow down, they accept the limitations that arise and see the transitions they are going through as opportunities to ground themselves in a deeper sense of self and a greater wisdom. . . . They are able to enjoy life more than they did when they were young because they have a deeper understanding of it.

Maybe you, too, have known someone like this. These are people who do not conform to a youth-obsessed culture's expectations of what their latter years will be like. Instead, their lives come to enact an entirely different vision of aging. No longer so driven by the desires that shaped the first part of their lives, their lives become more about meaning than about ambition, more about intimacy than about achieving. They experience the second half of their life as a time of deepening creativity and ripening of the soul.

John Robbins,
Healthy at 100: The Scientifically Proven Secrets of
the World's Healthiest and Longest-Lived Peoples, *2006.*

Customized Diets

The one-size-fits-all approach to diet is giving way to a more personalized approach. "General guidelines don't motivate people to change," says David Heber, director of UCLA's Center for Human Nutrition. "Personalized nutrition gets people to pay attention." That's why nutritionists are happy to see that fad diets are fading as research demonstrates that our genes have a lot to do with the way we should eat. Preliminary studies have shown, for example, that the amount of fat, protein and carbohydrates we choose to eat may be determined by our genes. Researchers have even identified a gene linked to heart disease. "The data we keep accumulating show the possibility is there," says Jose Ordovas, director of the Nutrition and Genomics Laboratory at the Jean Mayer USDA [U.S. Department of Agriculture] Human Nutrition Research Center on Aging at Tufts [University in Boston]. "But I would compare it to Windows 1.0. We're not nearly at Windows Vista." Still, some programs, including the Risk Factor Obesity Program at UCLA, take into account individual characteristics such as body fat, metabolism, blood pressure and cholesterol levels, as well as factors associated with heart disease, cancer and other chronic conditions. As Ordovas says, "It's the fine-tuning that's the difference between good and bad aging."

The days of a structured exercise regimen have given way to "active living every day," says Ruth Ann Carpenter, director of dissemination and advocacy at the Cooper Institute, a non-profit fitness and health organization in Dallas [Texas]. Although more than 60% of the U.S. adult population is considered sedentary, research shows that those who get the recommended 30 minutes of exercise per day—even if it's by parking farther from their destination, taking the stairs instead of the elevator, walking the dog or gardening—get the same health benefits as someone who participates in a conventional fitness activity for the same amount of time. "A big part of a successful exercise plan is enjoyment," explains Carpenter. That idea is just beginning to impact fitness trends. "There's no longer a sense that people want a quick fix or need to look like Miss Universe," says Carol Espel, national director of group fitness and Pilates for the [New York–based] Equinox Fitness clubs. "People don't want to show up and dial in their workout. They want a skill, to learn a technique, to master something while using their brain." Espel says getting a workout can be the healthy side effect, not the primary focus.

> "Our findings show that cognitive impairment without dementia affects a very large segment of the elderly population."

A Significant Number of Seniors Experience Decreased Mental Function

Brenda L. Plassman et al.

The following article uses results from a mental-capacity study—centering on 856 subjects over age seventy and carried out by researchers from Duke University Medical Center and the Universities of Michigan, Southern California, and Iowa—to argue that significant mental decline is more common than suspected in older adults. The authors assert that more than 20 percent of individuals in their seventies and older have cognitive impairment that, though not as serious as actual dementia, may progress to such. Brenda L. Plassman, lead author of this selection, is with the Department of Psychiatry and Behavioral Sciences at Duke University Medical Center.

Brenda L. Plassman et al. "Prevalence of Cognitive Impairment Without Dementia in the United States," *Annals of Internal Medicine*, vol. 148, no. 6, March 18, 2008, pp. 427–428, 432–433. Reproduced by permission.

As you read, consider the following questions:

1. How many seventy-year-old or older individuals were considered for the study, according to the viewpoint?

2. What percentage of cognitive impairment do the authors believe is due to chronic medical conditions?

3. What factors do the authors suggest might possibly have biased the study's results?

Cognitive impairment that does not reach the threshold for dementia diagnosis is associated with increased risk for progression to dementia in most studies, with progression rates of 10% to 15% per year compared with 1% to 2.5% among cognitively healthy older adults. However, even among those without dementia, cognitive impairment contributes to decreased quality of life, increased neuropsychiatric symptoms, and increased disability, as well as increased health care costs. All of these negative outcomes make accurate national estimates of the prevalence of cognitive impairment without dementia essential for determining the full societal impact of cognitive impairment on patients, families, and health care programs. However, previous estimates of the prevalence of this condition from regional and non-U.S. samples have varied from 3% to 29%, a range that is most likely due to differences in diagnostic criteria and sample characteristics. Estimates of the total number of people with cognitive impairment without dementia in the United States are not available.

The First Population-Based Study of Cognitive Impairment Without Dementia

We conducted ADAMS (Aging, Demographics, and Memory Study) to determine the national prevalence of dementia and cognitive impairment without dementia in the United States. . . . In this article, we report prevalence rates from what we believe to be the first population-based study of cognitive impairment without dementia to include individuals from all regions of the country, as well as rates of progression from cognitive impairment without dementia to dementia and death.

We drew the ADAMS sample from the larger HRS (Health and Retirement Study), an ongoing nationally representative cohort study of individuals born before 1954 that was designed to investigate the health, social, and economic implications of aging in the U.S. population. The HRS began in 1992, and the current sample includes approximately 22,000 participants.

The ADAMS sample began with a stratified random subsample of 1770 individuals age 70 years or older from 5 cognitive strata based on participants' scores on a self-reported or proxy-reported cognitive measure from the most recent HRS interview (either 2000 or 2002). We further stratified the 3 highest cognitive strata by age (age 70 to 79 years vs. ≥80 years) and sex to ensure adequate numbers in each subgroup. . . . The ADAMS initial assessments occurred between July 2001 and December 2003, on average, 13.3 months after the HRS interview. Thus, participants were 71 years of age or older at the initial assessment.

Collecting Information and Modeling Probability

As part of the ADAMS assessment, proxies (usually a spouse or adult child) provided information about the participant's cognitive and functional decline, neuropsychiatric symptoms, and medical history. Use of proxies to collect this information is preferred, because self-reporting of this type of information may not be reliable, particularly among cognitively impaired individuals. . . .

A total of 856 individuals, 56% of the nondeceased target sample, participated in all phases of the dementia assessment.

"Grandpa's at that wonderful age when he can't remember if he already gave me my allowance," cartoon by *Harley Schwadron*, CartoonStock.com.

A major concern in ADAMS, as in similar population-based studies, is the potential for selective nonparticipation to bias prevalence estimates. However, because the ADAMS sample was derived from the HRS sample, a wide range of health and social information was available to assess and correct for potential selection bias due to nonparticipation in our sample. Using logistic regression [a means of calculating probability of an occurrence, usually by means of risk factors, or "covariates"] we modeled the probability that a sample individual participated in the ADAMS assessment as a function of covariates, such as age, sex, education, marital status, HRS cognition scores, nursing home residency, and indicators of past or existing major health conditions. We used the results of this response propensity analysis to develop nonresponse adjustments to the ADAMS sample selection weights. We then constructed population sample weights to take into account the probabilities of selection in the stratified sample design and to adjust for differential nonparticipation in ADAMS. . . .

About 5.4 Million Individuals Affected

The ADAMS has produced the first prevalence estimates of cognitive impairment without dementia and its major subtypes in a nationally representative sample in the United States. We estimate that 22.2% (about 5.4 million) of individuals in the United States age 71 years or older have cognitive impairment without dementia. These results suggest that the number of individuals with cognitive impairment without dementia in the United States is about 70% higher than that with dementia, based on our previous estimate of 3.4 million individuals in this age group in the United States with dementia. In the 71- to 79-year age group, 16% had cognitive impairment without dementia, whereas an additional 5% had dementia, suggesting that more than 1 of 5 individuals in this age group has cognitive impairment. Overall, individuals with cognitive impairment without dementia progressed to dementia at a rate of about 12% per year, but the annual rate of progression ranged from 2% to 20% across the various subtypes. The overall annual mortality rate was 8%, but it ranged from 0% to almost 15% across the various subtypes of cognitive impairment without dementia.

To date, no other estimates of the number of individuals with cognitive impairment without dementia in the United States are available to compare with these ADAMS estimates. Reviews often report the prevalence of cognitive impairment without dementia as ranging from 5% to 29%. Even so, estimates from the few available U.S. regional and Canadian samples report prevalence rates for cognitive impairment without dementia of 17% to 23%, closely bracketing the ADAMS estimate of 22.2%. Selected European population studies using different criteria for cognitive impairment without dementia report prevalence rates ranging from 21% to 27%.

Individuals Without Dementia Less Likely to Be Tested

Our findings suggest that cognitive impairment without dementia due to chronic medical conditions accounts for about 24% of all cognitive impairment without dementia in the United States. Previous research suggests that individuals with this condition are less likely to be seen at university clinics for memory disorders and may be excluded from clinical trials even though numerous epidemiologic studies have reported an association between some of these medical conditions (for example, diabetes and heart failure) and cognitive impairment. This large group may be the most underdiagnosed subtype of cognitive impairment without dementia, and their cognitive impairment may get relatively less attention from medical providers as the treatment of their primary health issues takes priority.

Previous epidemiologic research has noted variation across subtypes of cognitive impairment without dementia in rates of prevalence, progression to dementia, and mortality, which shows that cognitive impairment without dementia is a heterogeneous condition with multiple causes. Accurately distinguishing among subtypes of cognitive impairment without dementia will become more important as effective treatments are developed.

No Single Set of Criteria Available

No single set of consensus criteria for cognitive impairment without dementia is currently available. This has led to debate about the appropriate classification of individuals in the zone between normal cognition and dementia, which has implications for the interpretation of our results. Whereas some research groups have pointed to clinical, neuropathologic, and functional neuroimaging evidence to suggest that individuals with mild impairment constitute a distinct group in transition from normal cognition to dementia, others have suggested that those with mild impairment actually have early dementia. When we assessed the effect on the prevalence rate of dementia after classifying some participants with cognitive impairment without dementia to have had dementia at baseline, the prevalence rate for Alzheimer disease increased but was still substantially less than the higher estimates of 4.5 million and 5 million with Alzheimer disease reported by other studies.

Limitations of This Study

Limitations of ADAMS include possible response bias from a participation rate that was lower than we hoped for. To minimize response bias, we used archived information from past interviews to develop response propensity models and associated weighting adjustments. The range of available measures used in these models probably captured most of the major factors that could statistically significantly contribute to selection bias in our population estimates. As proof of this, our calculations showed that the total size of the population age 71 years or older in 2002 using the ADAMS sample weights closely matched the population estimates from the U.S. Census Bureau. Diagnostic errors may have occurred because of inaccuracies in the diagnostic criteria and in the assignment of the diagnosis by the consensus panel. The criteria for both cognitive impairment without dementia and its subtypes are in the developmental stages and require further validation. The diagnostic subtypes are loosely defined and rely substantially on clinical judgment. They may not truly reflect different causes or predict prognosis. However, just as the criteria for several other neuropsychiatric conditions have evolved over time, we expect that these criteria will be refined after additional investigation to further characterize clinical phenotypes [physical and behavioral traits] identification of specific biological markers, and longer follow-up periods to determine outcomes. We attempted to minimize variability in the assignment of the clinical diagnosis within this study by using assessment teams based at a single site that used methods established in our previous epidemiologic studies and by using 1 expert case review panel.

Significant Numbers Affected

Our findings show that cognitive impairment without dementia affects a very large segment of the elderly population. The heterogeneous presentation of symptoms and outcomes in these individuals implies varied underlying causes that may provide opportunities for prevention strategies on several fronts. Prevention strategies may include programs targeting stroke prevention, cardiovascular risk factor reduction (for example, exercise and nutrition), and similar proactive approaches to education and management of chronic medical conditions. Positive gains from these strategies may reduce the prevalence of cognitive impairment without dementia and may have marked benefits for public health. Future longitudinal research using data from HRS and ADAMS, as well as from other studies of aging, may identify interventions that reduce the prevalence of cognitive impairment without dementia and benefit patients, families, and our aging society.

| "The story about aging is not a simple story of decline. Rather, it is a qualified and more nuanced story than the one often told."

Overall, Mental Function Does Not Lessen with Age

Laura L. Carstensen

Laura L. Carstenen, in the following viewpoint, argues that much supposed loss of mental function in seniors is exaggerated and can be compensated for. While, other things being equal, younger minds are quicker to process new information and create innovations than older minds, research shows that almost anyone's cognitive performance can be improved through memory strategies and by setting aside the idea that "all seniors have poor memories," she says. To meet growing needs of the aging population, Carstensen advocates further research of seniors' mental and other capabilities. Carstensen is a psychology professor at Stanford University and director of the Stanford Center on Longevity.

Laura L. Carstensen, "Growing Old or Living Long: Take Your Pick," *Issues in Science and Technology*, vol. 23, no. 2, Winter 2007, pp. 41–44, 50. Copyright © 2007 National Academy of Sciences. Reproduced by permission.

As you read, consider the following questions:

1. What does Carstensen consider to be the primary reason for increased life expectancy?
2. According to Carstensen, in what areas is mental decline most evident with age?
3. In Thomas Hess's deficits-in-performance study, cited by Carstensen, what was the primary difference between the three groups tested?

The 20th century witnessed two profound changes in regions of the world where people are well educated and science and technology flourish: Life expectancy nearly doubled, and fertility rates fell dramatically. As a result, individuals and populations are aging.

Virtually all educated people are aware of the graying of the United States, yet relatively few are as aware of its implications for science, technology, and human culture. Longer life is a remarkable achievement, but now we need to apply what we are learning in the natural and social sciences to redesign human culture to accommodate long lives. We need to find cures for Alzheimer's disease and arthritis, develop technologies that render many age-related frailties such as poor balance invisible in the way eyeglasses now compensate for presbyopia [an eye condition that comes on with age making upclose focusing difficult], and begin seriously rethinking cultural norms, such as the timing of education and retirement.

Longevity Is a Byproduct of Better Living Conditions

Longevity is the largely unexpected consequence of improvements in general living conditions. Genetically speaking, we are no smarter or heartier than our relatives were 10,000 years ago. Nonetheless, in practical terms we are more biologically fit than our great-grandparents. [Economic historian and Nobel laureate] Robert Fogel and his colleague Dora Costa coined the term "technophysio evolution" to refer to improvements in biological functioning that are a consequence of technological advances. They point out that technologies developed mostly in the past [twentieth] century vastly improved the quality and sustainability of the food supply. Subsequent improvements in nutrition were so dramatic that average body size increased by 50% and life expectancy doubled. The working capacity of vital organs greatly improved. Breakthroughs in manufacturing, transportation, energy production, and communications contributed further to improvements in biological functioning. Medical technology now enables full recovery from accidents or illnesses that were previously fatal or disabling.

Even technophysio evolution may be too narrow a term. Just as dramatic as the technologies are the acceptance and incorporation of the advances into everyday life. Not only was pasteurization discovered, it was implemented in entire populations. Not only were insights into the spread of disease observed in laboratories, community-wide efforts to dispose of waste were systematically undertaken. Not only was child development better understood, child labor laws prevented little ones from working long hours in unsafe conditions. Culture changed. Life expectancy increased because we built a world that is exquisitely attuned to the needs of young people.

Culture Must Become Responsive to Elders' Needs

Remember, however, that advances of the 20th century did not aim to increase longevity or alleviate the disabling conditions of later life. Longer life was the byproduct of better conditions for the young. The challenge today is to build a world that is just as responsive to the needs of very old people as to the very young. The solutions must come from science and technology. Unlike evolution by natural selection, which operates across millennia, improvements in functioning due to technological advances can occur in a matter of years. In fact, given that the first of the 77 million Baby Boomers turned 60 in 2006, there is no time to waste. To the extent that we effectively use science and technology to compensate for human frailties at advanced ages, the conversation under way in the nation changes from one about old age to one about long life, and this is a far more interesting and more productive conversation to have.

Psychological Science and Longevity

In psychology, as in most of the biological and social sciences, research on aging has focused mostly on decline. And it has found it. The aging mind is slower and more prone to error when processing information. It is less adept at considering old information in novel ways. Memory suffers. In particular, working memory—the ability to keep multiple pieces of information in mind while acting on them—declines with age. The ability to inhibit extraneous information when attempting to focus attention becomes impaired. Declines are especially evident on tasks that require effortful processing that relies on attention, inhibition, working memory, prospective memory, and episodic memory.

These changes begin in a person's 20's and 30's and continue at a steady rate across the adult years. They occur in virtually everyone, regardless of sex, race, or educational background. In all likelihood, these effects are accounted for by age-related changes in the efficiency of neurotransmission.

Despite these changes in cognitive processing, the subjective experience of normal aging is largely positive. By experiential and objective measures, most older people remain active and involved in families and communities. The majority of people over 90 live independently. The National Research Council [a subsidiary of the nonprofit National Academy of Sciences in Washington, D.C.] report *The Aging Mind: Opportunities in Cognitive Research* observed that performance on laboratory tasks does not map well onto everyday functioning. The committee speculated that much of the discrepancy occurs because people spend most of their time engaged in well-practiced activities of daily routines where new learning is less critical. Research shows that in areas of expertise, age-related decline is minimal until very advanced ages.

Older People Are Capable of Learning

Arguably even more interesting and important is growing evidence that performance—even on basic processes such as semantic or general memory—improves under certain conditions. One of the first such studies was reported by [psychologists] Paul Baltes and Reinhold Kliegl in 1992. They demonstrated rather striking improvement in memory with practice. Baltes and Kliegl first enlisted younger and older people's participation in a study of memory training. They assessed the participants' baseline performance and, as expected, younger participants outperformed older participants. However, after this initial assessment, participants attended a series of training sessions in which they were taught memory strategies such as mnemonics. They found that older people's memory performance benefited from practice so much that after only a few practice sessions, older people performed as well as younger people had before they had practiced. Younger people's performance also improved with training, of course, so at no point in the study did older people outperform younger people at the same point in training. But the fact that older people improved to the equivalent of untrained younger people speaks to the potential for improvement.

More recently, scientists have begun to investigate social conditions that also may affect performance. [Psychology professor] Tammy Rahhal and her colleagues reasoned that because there are widespread beliefs in the culture that memory declines with age, tests that explicitly feature memory may invoke performance deficits in older people. They compared

Brain Myths

Brain Myth: The brain powers down as you age.

In one sense, it's true. Brain-cell function does slow as you age, and it does become more difficult to store and retrieve things from short-term memory. But like good wine, aging can also make a well-used brain better. As you age, your brain cells build stronger and better connections, which means that as you experience events, you can do more crosslinking, cross-indexing, and cross-connecting. And as you age, the practice, experiences, and insights gained over time come into play in entirely new and creative ways. . . .

Brain Myth: Once brain cells are lost, they're gone forever.

Research carried out since the late 1980s has shown that not only can the brain make new cells (although it's yet to be demonstrated that they do anything), it can also "coax" other cells to take over the function of damaged or dead cells when they are stimulated and trained to do so. Recently, there has been an explosion in the number of research projects and programs on retraining the brain, which help people compensate for cognitive and functional loss by teaching them how to use different parts of their brains, training them to use all their senses to access the information stored in damaged cells, and teaching them "spaced retrieval" strategies that enable them to remember information for longer and longer periods.

Robert Palmer with Eileen Beal,
Age Well! A Cleveland Clinic Guide, *2007.*

memory performance in younger and older people under two experimental conditions. In one, the instructions stressed the fact that memory was the focus of the study. The experimenter repeatedly stated that participants were to "remember" as many statements from a list as they could and that "memory" was the key. In the second condition, experimental instructions were identical except that the instructions emphasized learning instead of memory. Participants were instructed to "learn" as many statements as they could. Once again, rather remarkable effects were observed. Age differences in memory were found when the instructions emphasized memory, but no age differences were observed in the condition that instead emphasized learning.

The Role of Motivation and Expectations

In another study, Thomas Hess [professor of psychology at North Carolina State University] and his colleagues documented deficits in performance when participants were reminded about declines that accompany aging before they began the experiment. In their study, participants read one of three newspaper articles before completing a memory task. One simulation reaffirmed memory decline and raised concerns that it may be worse than previously documented. In another condition, participants read a simulated article that described research findings suggesting that memory may improve with age. The third article was memory-neutral. In Hess's study, younger people outperformed older people in all three conditions, but the gap was significantly reduced in participants who read the positive account of memory. Most important, Hess's team identified a potential mediator of these performance differences. Participants were required to write down as many words as they could remember and those who had read the positive account about memory were more likely to use an effective memory strategy, called semantic clustering, in which similar words are grouped together. These strategic efforts were not observed in participants who were reminded of age deficits. Such findings point to the role of motivation in cognitive performance.

Thus, although there is ample evidence for cognitive deficits with age, the story about aging is not a simple story of decline. Rather, it is a qualified and more nuanced story than the one often told. Even in areas where there is decline, there is also growing evidence that performance can be improved in relatively simple ways. This poses a challenge to psychology to identify conditions where learning is well maintained, to find ways to frame information in ways best absorbed, and ultimately to improve cognitive and behavioral functioning by drawing on strengths [and] minimizing weaknesses. . . .

The Future of Longevity Science

Human need is the basis for virtually all of science. If we rise to the challenge of an aging population by systematically applying science and technology to questions that improve quality of life in adulthood and old age, longer-lived populations will inspire breakthroughs in the social, physical, and biological sciences that will improve the quality of life at all ages. Longevity science will reveal ways to improve learning from birth to advanced ages and to deter age-related slowing in cognitive processing. Longevity science will draw enormously on insights about individuals' genomic predispositions and the environmental conditions that trigger the onset of disease, as well as identifying genetic differences in individuals who appear resilient despite bad habits. Longevity science will help us understand how stress slowly but surely affects health. Most of the challenges of longer-lived populations will require interdisciplinary collaborations. Psychological science must be a part of this process.

Periodical Bibliography

The following articles have been selected to supplement the diverse views presented in this chapter.

Advocate	"The Age-Old Question," December 4, 2007.
Stephen Armstrong	"Care Revolutionaries," *New Statesman,* February 11, 2008.
Sharon Begley	"The Upside of Aging," *Wall Street Journal (Eastern Edition),* February 16, 2007.
Toni Calasanti	"A Feminist Confronts Ageism," *Journal of Aging Studies,* April 2008.
Catherine G. Ferrario, Florida J. Freeman, Gaile Nellett, and Jeanne Scheel	"Changing Nursing Students' Attitudes About Aging: An Argument for the Successful Aging Paradigm," *Educational Geronotology,* January 2008.
Carol A. Gosselink, Deborah L. Cox, Sarissa J. McClure, and Mary L.G. De Jong	"Ravishing or Ravaged: Women's Relationships with Women in the Context of Aging and Western Beauty Culture," *International Journal of Aging & Human Development,* 2008.
Margaret Morganroth Gullette	"What Exactly Has Age Got to Do with It? My Life in Critical Age Studies," *Journal of Aging Studies,* April 2008.
Bernadine Healy	"Young Brains, Beware," *U.S. News & World Report,* December 5, 2005.
Paula Ketter	"Cognitive Decline Need Not Be Part of Aging," *T&D,* January 2008.
Christine Larson	"Keeping Your Brain Fit," *U.S. News & World Report,* February 11, 2008.
Abigail Trafford	"An Older, Wiser Revolution," *Washington Post,* March 22, 2005.
————	"A Prejudice that Kills," *Washington Post,* July 4, 2006.

CHAPTER 2

How Should
Government and
Business Help Support
the Aging Population?

Chapter Preface

For more than seventy years, Americans have relied on the U.S. government to help fund their retirement years through Social Security. But since the money comes from taxes paid by the currently employed, nearly every analyst agrees that the system will soon either need a serious overhaul, or collapse upon itself. Not only is the vast majority of the population now living well beyond the traditional retirement age of sixty-five, but with the enormous baby boomer population now moving into that age bracket, the workers-to-retirees ratio is expected to shrink by more than a third within two decades, perhaps putting an unsustainable strain on available resources. Other programs, from Medicare to corporate pensions, are dreading the same pinch.

What can be done? "There are only three real solutions to Social Security's rapidly approaching fiscal problems," says David C. John, Senior Research Fellow at the Thomas A. Roe Institute for Economic Policy Studies, "raise taxes, reduce spending, or make the current payroll taxes work harder by investing them through some form of personal retirement account (PRA). Establishing PRAs is the only solution that will also give future retirees the option to receive an improved standard of living in retirement." By thus "privatizing" Social Security, the argument goes, the tax strain on workers would be reduced and they would also be contributing to their own future support, not just that of current retirees.

Other people argue that privatization would make little practical difference: First, taxes would have to be raised immediately to keep up payments to those already receiving Social Security, putting an additional financial burden on current workers; and second, with the government borrowing Social Security payments from the same system that funded the PRAs, no ultimate increase in retirement savings would result—perhaps savings would even decrease, considering the required fees for many private accounts. Raising taxes may well be the only workable solution.

Still others say there is no workable solution—that perhaps the only solution is to eliminate Social Security altogether. Many others would rather do away with retirement, arguing that people who are still capable of working have no right to expect strangers to support them solely because of their age. In fact, many people in their sixties are finding that, even with Social Security, they cannot afford to retire—at least not on the standard of living they were accustomed to. Social Security income rarely equals the salary level achieved during an actual career, according to this argument, and nearly 15 percent of people in their fifties have not put away enough money of their own for retirement. Some observers blame Social Security itself for that phenomenon, claiming that the system fuels the irresponsibility that always accompanies a sense of entitlement.

Other people insist that it is hardly fair, having taken as Social Security payments some of the income that could have gone into baby boomers' savings, to now deny them any similar support.

This chapter explores some of the issues surrounding Social Security, government policies, and retirement.

> "We have a high moral obligation to en-
> sure that future generations continue to
> benefit from this safety net and social
> contract. . . . To do this, we must fix
> the system."

Government Benefits for Retirees Must Be Prescrved

Chuck Hagel

*In the following viewpoint, U.S. senator Chuck Hagel (R-NE)
explains the reasoning behind his Social Security Reform Bill, introduced to Congress in March 2005, which failed to pass. Considering the expected economic impact when the largest age segment of the U.S. population—the 77 million baby boomers—
becomes eligible for Social Security and Medicare, and arguing
the necessity of such programs to reduce poverty, Hagel advocates
raising the age of eligibility for full benefits, encouraging citizens
to work more years before retiring, and taking increased life expectancy into account. Hagel plans to retire from the Senate in
2009.*

Chuck Hagel, "Saving Social Security," *USA Today Magazine*, vol. 133, no. 2720, May
2005, pp. 10–12. Copyright © 2005 Society for the Advancement of Education. Reproduced by permission.

As you read, consider the following questions:

1. What third component does Hagel favor adding to average income and the wage index as a factor in determining an individual's base Social Security benefit?

2. According to Hagel, by what year will more money be paid out of Social Security than is coming in?

3. Whose Social Security benefits would not have been affected by Hagel's proposed Social Security Reform Bill?

Social Security has been one of the most important and successful government programs in U.S. history. Almost every American family over the last 70 years has been touched by it. In signing the Social Security Act of 1935, Pres. Franklin Roosevelt declared, "None of the sums of money paid out to individuals in assistance or insurance will spell anything approaching abundance, but they will furnish that minimum necessity to keep a foothold and that is the kind of protection Americans want."

A fundamental point that Roosevelt made was that Social Security was not intended to replace the personal responsibility of individuals saving for and preparing for their own retirements. Social Security never was supposed to be a substitute for a retirement or savings plan. It is a safety net, an insurance contract that protects the most vulnerable in our society from falling into poverty. However, Social Security is actuarially unsustainable with its present commitments to future generations.

Retirement of the Baby Boomers Will Have Enormous Impact

The baby boom generation [those Americans born between 1946 and 1964] has been the largest and most productive workforce in the history of man. The impending retirement of 77,000,000 boomers will impact every aspect of our economy, government, and society: Medicare and Medicaid; health care;

the workforce; and the U.S.'s competitive position in a world filled with countries with workers much younger than ours.

The baby boom generation has a moral obligation to ensure that tomorrow's workers do not have to bear the increasingly heavy burden of providing the retirement resources for future generations. That is why Social Security must be reformed. It is a 1935 model trying to operate in a 21st century world. It soon will be incapable of delivering the promises and resources that it was built to provide.

Federal Reserve Board Chairman Alan Greenspan, speaking before the House Budget Committee, [in 2005] urged Congress to act on modernizing entitlement programs "sooner rather than later." He warned that, unless we act now, meeting the huge unfunded liabilities facing our entitlement programs will cause "severe" economic consequences for the nation. He is dead-on correct.

Medicare and Social Security Will Soon Be Financially Unsustainable

The U.S.'s largest entitlements—Social Security, Medicare, and Medicaid—are on a trajectory that cannot be sustained. For Fiscal Year 2006, the Congressional Budget Office maintains that 64% of the 2.5 trillion dollar budget will be obligated to mandatory spending, of which 42% is for these three programs. Those are tax dollars that are committed money that cannot be used for anything else. Each year, the percentage of the budget obligated to funding entitlement grows larger and larger. The current unfunded liability for Social Security over the 75-year horizon of the Social Security Administration uses to calculate benefits and expenditures is four trillion dollars. Medicare's unfunded liability is nearly 28 trillion dollars. This is in addition to America's current national debt of 7.5 trillion dollars.

Medicare costs are growing faster than any other government or entitlement program. As health care costs continue to rise, coupled with the growing number of retirees, it will put more and more pressure on the Federal budget and squeeze out money from important discretionary government programs like education, roads, parks, and housing. Last Congress [in 2003] we passed an enormous expansion of Medicare. I voted against it. I thought it was bad policy and would add hundreds of billions of dollars to an already unsustainable program.

The Social Security system is not in crisis today, but there clearly is one on the horizon. In 2017, more money will be paid out of Social Security than comes in. In 2041, the Social Security Trust Fund will be insolvent. Beyond the next 75 years, there is a black hole of unfunded liability for future generations. The longer nothing is done, the more difficult it will be to protect Social Security and the promise our government made to future generations. This reality is daunting, but there is good news. The system can be fixed. It is within our power to preserve the social safety net of this nation. It has been done before. In 1983, Pres. Ronald Reagan worked with Congress to make tough choices and extend the life of Social Security.

Dealing with this problem now means facing less dramatic and difficult choices down the road. The earlier we confront the reality of the coming crisis, the more options we will have to come up with a wise and sustainable course of action.

Reforming the System

Allow me now to lay out the main points of my Social Security Reform Bill. It would make changes to Social Security only for those Americans under the age of 45 by providing the option of voluntary personal accounts. This is good policy for the long-term viability of Social Security and for individuals. Government should be about empowering individuals and enhancing personal freedoms and their futures. Personal accounts help do this.

It Is Not About Solvency

Social Security reform must be properly understood. It is not about achieving solvency; it is about improving the system so that it offers a better deal for younger Americans through personal savings accounts. Focusing on solvency will lead inevitably to tax increases and benefit cuts. Focusing on personal retirement accounts improves the chance of enacting sound public policy that also makes the system solvent.

Mike Pence, "No New Taxes,"
Wall Street Journal, *January 13, 2007.*

For those under 45, there would continue to be a guaranteed benefit from the Social Security Trust Fund. Under any reform plan, Americans still need the security of knowing that the portion of their benefits that come from the traditional system will be guaranteed. Survivor and disability benefits would continue to be guaranteed as they currently are.

Social Security provides benefits for more than 6,000,000 spouses and children of bread-winners who died prematurely or became disabled. For these families, benefits should not be touched. I know something about this. When I was 16 years old, my father died. The benefits my mother received were critical in helping her raise four young boys. I well remember my mother's relief when that check arrived each month. We must remember that the first obligation of Social Security is to the most needy Americans.

Moreover, the bill does not raise taxes. We can fix Social Security without doing so. We need to begin reforming governmental programs so that they do not become so large and expensive that future taxpayers will be unable to pay for them.

Young wage earners and small businesses are the most vulnerable to tax increases, and they would be the ones most adversely affected. Additionally, whenever the costs of labor are increased, the U.S.'s competitive position in the world is damaged and job creation is made more difficult. This is not abstract economic theory. It is a reality that has an impact on every American. . . .

Remodeling Social Security for the Future

This country is blessed. The vast majority of Americans live healthier, longer lives than they did a few decades ago. Advances in medicine, education, and in personal health will continue to increase not only the length of these lives, but also the quality, providing opportunities for older Americans to remain healthy, vital, and productive members of the workforce.

When Social Security was created during the Great Depression of the 1930s, there were too many workers and not enough jobs. According to the Social Security Administration, in 1950, there were 16.5 workers per retiree. Incentives were created to move people out of the workforce. This dynamic is changing. Today, there are 3.3 workers for every retiree. In 25 years, there will be 2.1 workers for each retiree.

My bill makes three adjustments to Social Security that will ensure its solvency for future generations. First, it would raise the current full benefit retirement age by one year—from 67 to 68. Second, it would maintain the current early retirement age at 62, but would adjust benefits for those who choose that route. Currently, workers who retire early receive 70% of their full retirement benefits. The proposed bill would provide those early retirees with 63% of the traditional benefit.

Third, at present, an individual's base Social Security benefit is determined by two factors: average income over 35 years and the wage index. The bill adds a third component: life expectancy. Over the life of the program, Social Security benefit calculations never have been adjusted to reflect increased life expectancy. By factoring this in the rate of increase in benefit payments will be slowed. No other changes will be made to the annual Consumer Price Indexing of benefit increases.

In addition to solidifying Social Security's solvency these adjustments can help confront the challenges of increasing Medicare costs and shortages in the workforce. It is important to protect the option of early retirement, but the law needs to encourage individuals to stay in the workforce, not leave it. Medicare and Medicaid costs, as well as labor shortages, can be reduced significantly by keeping people healthy and productive and in the workforce.

Action Must Be Taken Now

The bill pays for these changes in Social Security by using the existing four trillion dollar unfunded liability to ensure the long-term health of the system. Doing nothing will mean that, at the end of 75 years, Social Security will have chewed up four trillion taxpayer dollars to keep the system solvent—and we still will have an insolvent program with trillions of dollars more unfunded liabilities staring us in the face. In recent testimony before the Senate, Greenspan insisted that Social Security's total unfunded liability could be as high as 10 trillion dollars over the life of the program.

All Americans need to ask tough questions about the future of Social Security. We need to begin the process of refining ideas to forge the best, most responsible policy for the future. Pres. George W. Bush deserves credit for making the modernization of Social Security a central part of his second term agenda.

We have a high moral obligation to ensure that future generations continue to benefit from this safety net and social contract we have with our citizens. In order to do this, we must fix the system.

I am 58 years old. I am at the front end of the baby boom generation. My daughter is 14 and my son is 12. I do not want to fail their generation. That means addressing these entitlement program issues now while we have time to do it in a responsible way.

This is a defining debate for today's leaders. Doing nothing is irresponsible and cowardly. It is in every American's interest to deal with this challenge. We can preserve, protect, and improve Social Security for all the future generations of Americans.

> "[Currently proposed] reforms can strengthen the financial position of the Social Security system, but they will do nothing to address the perverse incentives that the system generates."

Government Support for Retirees Discourages Personal Responsibility

Robin J. Klay and Todd P. Steen

In the following viewpoint, economics teachers Robin J. Klay and Todd P. Steen argue that the pending Social Security crisis is due not simply to a decreasing workers-to-retirees ratio, but largely to the sense of entitlement fostered by the current system. People have come to expect more support from the government than it can deliver, and thus are neglecting their personal responsibility to save for retirement. While the authors do not suggest abolishing Social Security altogether, they recommend more sweeping reforms than the standard proposals to reduce benefit increases and delay retirement. Klay and Steen teach at Hope College, in Holland, Michigan.

Robin J. Klay and Todd P. Steen, "Social Insecurity," *The Christian Century*, vol. 125, no. 3, February 12, 2008, pp. 31–33, 35. Copyright © 2008 Christian Century Foundation. All rights reserved. Reproduced by permission.

As you read, consider the following questions:

1. What do Klay and Steen cite as the major principles involved in effective financial preparation for retirement?

2. According to Klay and Steen, around what year will serious funding problems begin for the Social Security system?

3. What five suggestions do Klay and Steen make for reforming Social Security?

One of the greatest fruits of high productivity and rising incomes in a country like the U.S. is the financial ability people have to retire. This possibility was beyond the imagination of pre–World War II workers and is still far beyond the expectations of most people living in Third World countries. For most of human history, people simply worked until their bodies gave out and then depended on their children to care for them in the last years of life. Now, in advanced economies, retirement figures into almost everyone's expectations.

However, an expectation does not by itself create an adequate financial base for retirement, especially when the expectation is based—as it is in the U.S.—on substantial Social Security benefits. The fact that Social Security is in trouble has been trumpeted for more than a decade, but still no major reforms have been introduced to put things right. Because all potential reforms involve costs, politicians have deferred the necessary difficult decisions.

Social Security needs to be thought of in the larger context of retirement. Retirement is never a right. It is possible only through the fruit of productive labor, sacrificial saving, effective investment and responsible budgeting. Retirement depends on the willingness of families to routinely make sacrifices, setting aside some portion of their current income. Retirement also depends on firms using these savings to fund investment in new production facilities, better equipment, and research and development. The link between saving (by both governments and families) and retirement income is key to both a healthy economy and its ability to provide for senior citizens.

The Dangers of the Present Approach

The connection between saving and retirement earnings is most obvious for those who contribute to Individual Retirement Accounts. It is visible also to those who work in companies that provide pensions for which employee contributions are required.

The danger of delinking retirement income from saving is that families come to count on a *certain* future retirement (as with retirement plans that promise a specific benefit) and therefore tend to save less themselves. This has consequences both for the individual and the economy. For individuals, inadequate saving can make retirement difficult, if not impossible, should expectations about future benefits not be met. For the economy as a whole, less saving by individuals means slower growth in productivity. And slower growth in productivity means that there will be less growth in invested funds and so, in turn, less money available to fund retirement.

Even more dangerous to society is the disconnect that has arisen between the government's promises of Social Security benefits and its own commitment to save to provide these benefits. This weakness was built into the system from its inception in 1935. Originally, benefits paid to current retirees were to be funded exclusively from modest payroll taxes (1 percent of the first $3,000 earned) paid by both current employees and their employers. The initial beneficiaries of Social Security made no financial contributions into the system. During the first ten years of the system, the ratio of workers paying Social Security taxes to beneficiaries was more than 40 to 1. Given Depression rates of unemployment and the poverty conditions that prevailed, a commitment of benefits to the limited number of people who survived past the age of 65 seemed like the least society could do to help older workers and to honor their contributions.

Demographic Changes Will Soon Make Social Security Unworkable

Over the years, Social Security benefits have increased, as have the contributions required of workers. The tax rate for 2007 was 6.2 percent (this does not include the 1.45 percent tax rate paid for Medicare) on the first $97,500 of earnings, with this amount paid by both employees and employers. Benefits are now automatically adjusted yearly to offset the effect of inflation.

But demographic changes have rendered the Social Security system unsustainable in its current form. One important factor is the aging of the generation born between 1946 and 1964. In 2008 the first baby boomers can start retiring—at age 62—and receive partial benefits from Social Security. The baby boomers head into retirement at a time when birth rates have dropped—from 16.7 births per 1,000 people in 1990 to 14.2 births in 2007. In addition, life expectancy has increased over the past 40 years from an average of 70.8 years in 1970 to a projected lifespan of 78.5 years in 2010.

Because of these demographic changes, the number of workers for each beneficiary dropped from 5.1 in 1960 to 3.3 in 2006. This ratio is expected to decrease to 2.1 by 2030 and to 1.8 by 2080. As a result, the Social Security system faces serious funding shortfalls beginning around 2018 and continuing into the indefinite future. Given the huge gap between Medicare's current promises to seniors and its basis of funding, the future of retirement for the next generations is even bleaker.

The Decline of Personal Responsibility

How did we get into this fix? One reason is that people began to think of retirement funding as a right and primarily a public responsibility, and so—not surprisingly—started saving less. For more than a decade, American firms have been funding more and more of their capital investments—the key to economic growth—with money from foreign investors. Foreigners' willingness to place their savings in the U.S. is good for the U.S. economy in some ways, but it means that an increasing share of the fruits of economic growth goes to the foreign investors and are not available for funding the retirements of American workers.

Social Security taxes and benefit levels are not based on expected rates of return and risk levels for various savings instruments (as is the case in private savings portfolios). In fact, there is *nothing* in your Social Security portfolio. The federal government's excess revenues from Social Security receipts (since Social Security receipts are currently greater than expenditures) are not saved but instead are reallocated to fund other government programs. Meanwhile, the Social Security system continues to promise future benefits. These benefits are thus essentially IOUs from the federal government that must be paid in the future either by higher taxes or by further government borrowing.

The Limits of Social Security Reforms

The obvious and growing gap between Social Security's commitments and its expected future revenues means that Social Security should no longer be regarded as a riskless source of retirement income. In a poll taken by the *New York Times* in 2005, more than half of the respondents said they did not believe that the Social Security system will have the money to provide the promised benefits when they retire. It is common knowledge among economists, and politicians who are willing to look at the facts, that reforms are necessary. They must include some combination of smaller increases in benefits, higher payroll taxes and delayed retirement.

Such reforms can strengthen the financial position of the Social Security system, but they will do nothing to address the

Forcing Employees to Save for Retirement

The question of why people don't save more money is a hot topic in academic circles. A third of eligible 401(k) participants never sign up, and those who do typically don't put away enough. "We may have every intention of saving," says Brigitte Madrian, professor of public policy at Harvard University. "But most of us can't follow through."

That follow-through is what academics have been shedding light on lately, and the solution they've found is to do, well, nothing: If you make 401(k) enrollment automatic—new hires must opt out, not in—those who do nothing still save. In a recent analysis of companies that have adopted automatic enrollment, professors at Harvard and the University of Pennsylvania found that participation levels skyrocketed to as high as 96%. . . .

Letting your company automatically increase how much you put in your plan can cure low savings levels too. In a landmark experiment at one midwestern company, [University of Chicago behavioral finance expert Richard] Thaler and UCLA [University of California at Los Angeles] accounting professor Shlomo Benartzi found that automatic contribution hikes raised average savings rates from 3.5% to 11.6%.

The lesson from all these programs is that if you're forced to save, you probably will.

Penelope Wang, "What Works in Retirement Planning,"
Money, *October 2006.*

perverse incentives that the system generates. The powerful channels of individual responsibility are weakened when people are forced to "save" out of current income—through payroll taxes—but leave it to legislators with very short-term horizons to make decisions about retirement fund money.

Ways to Encourage Saving

Senior citizens are understandably tempted to pressure Congress to expand current Social Security benefits and to delay reforms, since the burden will be borne by another generation. Would these seniors have been willing to impose this burden on the next generation if it was obviously a direct burden on each of their own children? Not likely. Instead, they would probably have increased their personal savings to avoid becoming dependent for their retirement on their children's earnings.

However, whole generations have been led to believe that they are actually paying in Social Security taxes all that is needed to fully fund their future Social Security benefits. As a result, current retirees vote to maintain the right to receive benefits exceeding what they paid in, and beyond what the system can sustain.

It is precisely for these reasons that several proposals have been made to create personal savings accounts (a partial privatization of the system) whereby individual retirement incomes are linked to efforts to save. A middle-of-the-road proposal of this sort would take a portion of what is now collected as Social Security taxes and allocate them to personal retirement accounts, invested in a limited number of stock and bond instruments. The options would offer various risk/return values, and would be subject to government regulation. Individuals could choose the mix of risk to meet their own needs and values. Some, perhaps a majority, of Social Security taxes would continue to be collected to provide baseline retirement incomes to all workers.

Retirement Is Not a Right

Reforms such as higher taxes, lower benefits and delayed retirement are designed to put Social Security on a firm financial footing, so that the sheer passage of time does not force future payees and retirees into a crisis that would severely hurt both groups. Proposals to create personal savings accounts (PSAs), on the other hand, are designed to counter expectations that Social Security can be the primary source of retirement income. Because workers have the ability to choose the PSA portfolios that best fit their own circumstances, nobody will be led to believe that society owes them a retirement income. This design has operated successfully in a number of countries. In Chile, for example, national savings rates increased from 10 percent in 1986 to 29 percent in 1996. . . .

As stated previously, retirement is not a right. Its funding cannot be assured apart from rising U.S. productivity and greater fiscal responsibility. Neither Social Security reform nor partial privatization will come without cost. Both current and future generations must share these costs in a way that does not overburden particular cohorts. A fair approach to reform would include these features:

1. Maintaining benefit levels paid to soon-to-be and current retirees, because they have little or no earning lifetime left to save and invest for their retirement needs.

2. Lowering over time the net benefit increases promised to current and future retirees. This move usually includes reducing the inflation index by which the benefits are adjusted upward and making a greater share of benefits taxable.

3. Introducing progressive indexing to provide greater cost of living adjustments for the poorest retirees and less for others.

4. Raising the age of eligibility for Social Security benefits to reflect increased years of health and productivity.

5. Raising the income cap on Social Security tax payments (above the 2007 level of $97,500).

Introducing Change Slowly

These proposals have the virtue of introducing changes slowly and diffusely enough so that families can adjust their earning, spending and saving patterns. Their expectations will be better founded than they could ever be if government were to continue promising the impossible.

Several of the above proposed reforms also preserve one of the key objectives of Social Security: to ensure that even people with low earnings are able to retire with adequate benefits. To achieve this goal, higher-income workers already receive a lower return on the taxes that they pay than do lower income families. Raising the income cap would increase the existing progressivity of the system, as would applying greater cost-of-living benefit adjustments for families with lower earnings than to those with high earnings. Providing adequate retirement benefits to retirees whose lifetime earnings are low is clearly a matter of intergenerational justice.

By themselves, the sorts of reforms described above are not likely to fully solve the funding crisis that faces Social Security. In addition, they will do little to increase incentives for personal saving, which is ultimately needed to fund long-term economic growth and decent retirement incomes for future generations.

Americans Must Take More Active Roles in Personal Retirement Planning

As noted earlier, the advantage of introducing individual retirement accounts into the picture is to partially repair the present disconnect between individuals' savings and the political decisions about their eventual Social Security benefits. By itself, such a change would have the effect of calling Americans' attention to the fact that a retirement livelihood can never be just a promise. It requires saving. It demands that everyone become active in providing for his or her retirement through productive work, sacrificial saving—and limited expectations of what can be demanded of government.

Citizens who care about justice for future generations should demand answers on Social Security reform from the presidential candidates. The concerted effort needed for reform requires transcending party politics. We should be skeptical about candidates promising palatable short-term fixes that are aimed at attracting our votes. The long-term costs of that sort of politics will be enormous.

> "What makes addressing the aging population particularly challenging is that geriatrics . . . is an enormously complex kaleidoscope of medical procedures, government policy, and demographics."

The Medical System Is Not Prepared to Deal with an Aging Population

Conn Hallinan and Carl Bloice

The largest age segment of the world population is approaching retirement while geriatric doctors and caretakers are decreasing in numbers, notes the following viewpoint. According to the authors, compounding the potential medical crisis are negative attitudes toward old age that make it difficult to recruit new health-care workers. They also argue that medical professionals who treat physical complaints with little regard for individual needs are adding to health problems. Conn Hallinan is a columnist for the Foreign Policy in Focus think tank; Carl Bloice is a San Francisco writer who previously worked for a health-care union.

Conn Hallinan and Carl Bloice, "Coming of Age," *Registered Nurse*, vol. 103, no. 7, September 2007, pp. 10, 12–15. Reproduced by permission of the authors.

As you read, consider the following questions:

1. What types of skills, other than medical, does one professor of medicine cited in the viewpoint say geriatric workers should have?

2. According to the viewpoint, what is a geriatrician's typical annual salary, and how does this compare with other doctors' salaries?

3. What suggestions do the authors make for averting a serious shortage of proper health care for the elderly?

The earthquake that struck Kashiwazaki, Japan in July [2007] did more than smash up houses and kill 11 people. It exposed a fault line that had nothing to do with the island nation's unstable perch on the Pacific Ocean: All of the dead were over 65.

The great heat wave that battered Chicago 12 years ago [1995] made life about as unpleasant as it can get in that Midwest city, but for older people—most of whom were poor and nonwhite—it was a killer.

No one knows for sure how many people the heat wave that rolled across Europe in August 2003 killed, but in France the death toll was at least 15,000, the majority of them elderly.

Natural disasters have always had a way of shaking the glitter off systems and revealing the underlying fissures, be it inadequately maintained levees in New Orleans, or in the cases above, a systemic failure by social, political, and medical institutions to deal with a global demographic tsunami.

The Population Is Aging Throughout the World

By the year 2050, the number of humans 65 years or older will increase from a little over 600 million to two billion, two-thirds of whom reside in the Third World. "Aging is affecting virtually every country," United Nations General Secretary Ban Ki-moon told a Tokyo conference on aging this past April

[2007]. "The world has never seen such rapid, large, and ubiquitous growth in the number and proportion of elderly people."

In the United States, the number of people over 65—currently 35 million—will double by 2030, jumping from 13 percent of the population to 20 percent. And adults over 85 are currently the fastest growing demographic group in the U.S.

It's a different kind of boom for which we're not prepared. While the elderly population is climbing, the number of doctors and nurses who treat them is declining and the population of traditional caregivers is either stagnant or falling.

What makes addressing the aging population particularly challenging is that geriatrics, the branch of medicine that deals with the diseases, debilities, and care of older people, is an enormously complex kaleidoscope of medical procedures, government policy, and demographics. Problems or the wrong approach in any of these areas can lead to a train wreck.

Poverty and Isolation Prove Killers

In the aftermath of the 1995 Midwest heat wave, researchers found that it was not so much the temperature that killed people, but poverty, isolation, and fear. Many elders were too poor to afford air conditioning, they lived alone, and were too afraid to go out into the mean streets of Chicago. Isolated behind locked doors, they baked to death.

But tying together all the strands that make up the complex field of geriatrics is not a simple task. On one level, the infirmities of age like diabetes, arthritis, incontinence, and high blood pressure are medical conditions that can be treated with drugs. But as Dr. Claudia Landau, geriatric curriculum coordinator and an associate clinical professor of medicine at the University of California, Berkeley argues, when it comes to treating older people, "The medical model is not going to work."

Geriatrics, she says, needs doctors and nurses to be as much sociologists and anthropologists as medical workers. "They have to know whether their patients are poor or rich, they need to know the total terrain," said Landau. "If you don't attend to all of the elements, you are not going to care for old people very effectively."

The Trouble with the Current Medical Model

Yet currently, the medical model is relentlessly pushed by an avalanche of television ads on treatments for incontinence, diabetes, and high blood pressure—what researchers Dr. Carol L. Estes and Steven P. Wallace call the "commodification" of aging by a "medical-industrial complex" whose bottom line is money.

According to Joan Stanley, RN (registered nurse), senior director of education policy of the American Association of Colleges of Nursing, and Mathy Mezey, RN, a professor at New York University, "The care of older adults is now the number one business of the U.S. healthcare system, cutting across hospitals, home care and nursing homes."

"Adult diapers and drugs produce significant profits for their manufacturers, creating incentives to promote these products," write Estes and Wallace in the book *Social Injustice and Public Health*. "As a consequence, behavioral therapy, which is time consuming and not very profitable, is rarely used even though it is more effective."

For example, while loss of bladder control seems like one of aging's minor ailments, it is a major reason older people are institutionalized.

Exercise and Healthy Eating Are the Best Medicine

Studies show that conditions like incontinence, diabetes, and high blood pressure respond just as well to exercise and dietary regimes as they do to target drugs. Indeed, many times the drugs create the problems.

Dr. Wendel Brunner, now director of public health in Contra Costa County, Calif., recalled that when he was working in a clinic, "Old people would come in with bags of medicine. I would throw away most of it, and they would get better."

Treating older people takes certain skills that most general practitioners and specialists don't have. One of those skills is listening. "As we get older our homeostasis changes and doctors need to be tuned into that," said Landau. "You have to listen and take the time. You have to value communication." She calls this "cognitive medicine."

Is an older patient disoriented because he or she is losing their mental faculties, or because of depression? Do they have an infection? (Infections can be difficult to spot because older people tend not to run fevers.) Or are they on the wrong medication?

Drugs Can Create More Problems than They Cure

Doctors, for example, need to be particularly careful when prescribing drugs to elders. Diuretics are commonly prescribed for controlling high blood pressure, a chronic disease afflicting many older people. But if patients are not properly hydrated, diuretics can cause dizziness and falling. Of some 350,000 Americans who fall and break their hips each year, 40 percent will end up in nursing homes. A fifth will never walk again.

Side effects can be exacerbated when different doctors prescribe drugs without any centralized monitoring. "Multiple doctors prescribing multiple medicines cause multiple problems," said Brunner.

The flip side of overprescribing is the attitude among providers that there's nothing that can be done for elderly patients. Wallace and Estes found that many doctors tend to undertreat older patients, with some claiming "those over 80 should receive no curative treatments . . . because they have lived out their 'natural lives.'"

But a Harvard study found that when 90 year olds were put on Nautilus trainers their health improved. Landau recalled advocating physical therapy for older patients when she worked in a public health clinic, only to be accused of "torturing" them by some staff members. "I told them to humor me and lo, and behold, people got better," she said.

The Geriatric Profession Is Losing Doctors

A doctor or nurse certified in geriatrics is best trained to triage the health needs of elderly patients.

But out of the nation's 145 medical schools, only nine have geriatric departments, according to an April 2006 *New York Times* article. There is only one geriatric doctor for every 5,000 people in the United States. Fewer than 9,000 of the 650,000 doctors in the country are certified in geriatrics and fewer than 3 percent of medical students take courses in the subject. The number of U.S. geriatricians has dropped by one-third between 1998 and 2004.

"It's a problem," warned William Satariano, a professor of epidemiology's and community health at U.C. Berkeley School of Public Health and an expert on aging.

One reason why there are fewer geriatric doctors is that they are among the lowest paid in the profession. While radiologists and orthopedic surgeons average $400,000 a year, geriatricians average $150,000 a year. Brunner, however, is not overly sympathetic to this argument. "It is hard to feel bad about any doctor's income," he said. "The problem is not that we don't pay doctors enough."

The Number of Geriatric Nurses Is Shrinking

The shortage is not restricted to doctors. Only 720 of the 200,000 pharmacists in the U.S. have geriatric certification, and the situation is only slightly better for social workers.

Age Groups and Medical Care

Who is going to the doctor and hospital?

Patient age	1995	2005
Younger than 10 years old	15.5 %	13.5 %
10–19	8.8	8.5
20–29	10.4	8.8
30–39	14.2	10.5
40–49	13.5	13.8
50–59	10.4	14.8
60–69	10.7	12.3
70–79	11.0	10.6
80 years old and older	5.5	7.2

TAKEN FROM: Centers for Disease Control and Prevention,
Ambulatory Medical Care Utilization Estimates for 2005, June 2007.

Bonnie Martin, RN, NP [nurse practitioner], works in geriatrics in San Francisco and is a member of CNA/NNOC's [California Nurses Association/National Nurses Organizing Committee's] board of directors. She said the situation in nursing is "very similar." According to Martin, "very few RNs choose to work with the elderly and very few [nurse practitioners] attend geriatric programs." Much of the care for the elderly "is left to LVNs [licensed vocational nurses] and certified nursing care, in spite of the fact that the elderly need more complex nursing care than most other patient populations."

Stanley and Mezey argue that "evidence shows that older-person care delivered by nurses with specialized geriatric knowledge and skills improves outcomes" by improving patient assessment, reducing falls, and lowering costs.

Yet less than 1 percent of the 2.7 million nurses in the United States and Canada are certified in geriatrics and only 27 percent of nurses in baccalaureate programs have required classes in geriatric medicine.

Martin said the reason is that "nurses in [long-term care] tend to be paid significantly less, have fewer benefits, and are not considered among the nursing 'elite' an outgrowth of how little we value our elderly." . . .

Medicare Alternatives Are Expensive and Often Unscrupulous

The [George W.] Bush administration solution to the long-term care crises is to push market-driven schemes, like reverse mortgages and private long-term insurance. More than eight million Americans have purchased long-term care insurance, only to find that companies throw up one roadblock after another when it comes time to cash in. According to the state of California, one in four claims was denied in 2005. In the meantime, the industry has pulled in more than $50 billion in premiums.

As for reverse mortgages, they essentially wipe out one of the few assets working class people can pass on to their children.

According to AARP [American Association of Retired Persons], the advocacy group for retirees, this informal labor network is valued at anywhere from $275 to $350 billion a year, more than what Medicare costs. . . .

Finding solutions will not be easy and challenges a cohort of powerful lobbyists that run the gamut from pharmaceutical companies to insurance behemoths. On the other hand, the political power of seniors has grown over the past decade, and local and state governments, as well as the medical establishment, are coming under increasing pressure to respond to demands for improving elder care.

At least the outlines of a solution are out there.

The First Steps Toward a Solution

One is to end health disparity. "Everything links back to growing income inequality," said Brunner, and Satariano agreed that "the issue of disparity is critical."

Kay McVay, RN, and president emeritus of the California Nurses Association, says income is directly related to the quality of elder care. If patients don't have the money, they can "end up tied to a gurney or strapped in a wheelchair and stuck in the back of a facility."

Two is to create a nationwide healthcare system that coordinates care. "Single-payer healthcare would end the idea that you can make big profits off of old people," said McVay. "It establishes one standard of care for everyone, whether you are in an acute care facility or a long-term care facility. The only criteria should be: 'What does the patient need?'"

Three is to improve training. "Medical schools must train students to treat older Americans," said Brunner. "We have a right to make demands on our institutions," said Satariano. As Landau bluntly put it, "you have to teach geriatrics."

Four is designing communities and programs that take into account the ecology of aging. "When you are elderly you need not just medical attention and medications," said McVay. "You need good nutrition and exercise and things that challenge your mind. Otherwise it is just warehousing. It shouldn't be that way and needn't be that way."

Changing Our Attitudes Toward the Elderly

Mobilizing the medical profession; pushing federal, state, and local governments to stop turning a blind eye to the problem; and neutralizing the lobbying power of the "medical-industrial complex" will be a formidable task, and yet given the size of the constituencies involved, one that may not be as difficult as it initially looks.

In the end, it will also take a sea change in our attitude about elders, "who are not exactly revered," as Landau pointed out.

"I know it sounds sort of corny, but you have to have love and empathy. Aging is about loss—loss of independence, loss of mobility, eyesight, hearing, cognition. You need an approach that allows people to deal with loss in a collective, supportive way," she said.

> "Precisely because Medicare has become
> a public-private hybrid, it is uniquely
> situated to become the vehicle for seri-
> ous efforts to universalize health cover-
> age."

Medicare Is Changing to Meet the Needs of an Aging Population

Mark Schlesinger and Jacob S. Hacker

"Hybridizing" of Medicare—government's working with private insurance companies to provide services—has stirred considerable controversy. In the following viewpoint, Mark Schlesinger and Jacob S. Hacker argue in favor of the "new" approach to Medicare, on the grounds that it fosters increased competition and effectiveness, and is less subject to politics than a "pure government" program. Schlesinger is a health policy professor at the Yale School of Public Health. Hacker is a Yale professor of political science.

Mark Schlesinger and Jacob S. Hacker, "Secret Weapon: The 'New' Medicare as a Route to Health Security," *Journal of Health Politics, Policy and Law*, vol. 32, no. 2, April 2007, pp. 247–248, 259–262. Copyright © 2007 Duke University Press. All rights reserved. Used by permission of the publisher.

As you read, consider the following questions:

1. According to the authors, where did the Bill Clinton administration's Health Security Act fall short?

2. What do Schlesinger and Hacker consider to be the respective primary advantages of public and private insurance benefits?

3. What three concerns do Schlesinger and Hacker list as affecting policy makers' attitudes toward benefits programs?

A series of controversial changes over the past twenty years have altered Medicare from its original single-payer model.

The premise of this article is that these changes to Medicare, as mixed in their effects and contentious in their enactment as they have been, have actually increased the potential for expanding the program beyond its current base of eligibility. Precisely because Medicare has become a public-private hybrid, it is uniquely situated to become the vehicle for serious efforts to universalize health coverage. While the combination of public and private insurance may irritate ideological purists, it bolsters Medicare's public legitimacy. While these dualistic features have been challenging to administer in an even-handed fashion, they give the program sufficient flexibility to effectively address the needs of a diverse population and perform under the heterogeneous circumstances in which health care is delivered in the United States. Ironically, then, changes in Medicare mostly pushed by conservatives may be bringing into reach one of the oldest and most elusive goals of liberals: assuring access to affordable health insurance. Indeed, as improbable as it may seem at first, Medicare may be the *only* practical avenue for achieving health security for all Americans. . . .

Public-private hybrids are quite common. They are also diverse; some combine public financing with private administration, others reverse the roles, and others embody even more complex combinations of roles and responsibilities. To simplify our current discussion, we propose to focus our attention on one particular form of hybrid in which the public and private components of a program draw upon a common pool of resources and have an overlapping mission: in short, the type of hybrid program in which public and private components compete with one another. We will refer to this as a "competitive hybrid." This competition could take the form of individual beneficiaries choosing between public and private coverage (as is now the case for state Medicaid programs with voluntary enrollment in managed care plans) or of policy makers making this choice for an entire defined population (e.g., Medicaid programs with mandatory managed care enrollment or state children's health insurance programs [S-CHIPs] that are administered by either entirely public or entirely private insurance) in the context of a program that makes it possible to alter these choices over time.

Our central claim is that a competitive hybrid of public and private insurance significantly enhances the prospects of enacting universal health insurance coverage. As a corollary to this claim, we further predict that such a hybrid system will prove more resilient in its performance, although we also acknowledge that a health insurance system so designed will exhibit some persisting political and administrative tensions as well.

Enhanced Prospects or Program Enactment

A competitive hybrid of public and private insurance could draw upon broad public support that would transcend value cleavages and regional differences in Americans' conception of appropriate health security. Both liberals and conservatives could find aspects of the program attractive. When the public and private components compete for beneficiaries, those who fear either an impersonal government bureaucracy or unreli-

---

Competition Could Lower Medicare Costs

The Medicare prescription drug benefit [that went into effect in 2006, and provides for voluntary outpatient enrollment in a choice of plans for the purchase of medication] is so far costing less than anticipated, while seniors are getting more insurance options at lower prices. Lesson: Maybe private competition works.

This doesn't mean we're changing our minds that the new drug entitlement was a policy mistake at an estimated long-term cost of $8 trillion, give or take a trillion. But now that the program exists, it matters ... whether the seeds of market competition planted in the bill are allowed to grow.

Wall Street Journal, *October 4, 2006.*

---

able, market-driven practices can be comforted that alternatives exist. To be sure, mustering public support is not simply a matter of agglomerating [gathering together] elements that appeal to the supporters of public and private insurance. The components must fit together in a manner that is coherent for the public; this is where the [Bill] Clinton administration's HSA [Health Security Act of 1993, which was more than thirteen hundred pages long] fell short, since its combination of rights-based and market-driven elements never made sense to most American voters.

Hybrid Programs Appeal to Interest Groups

The prospects for competitive hybrids of public and private insurance are equally enhanced by their implications for political elites. Hybrid programs offer a means of addressing the heterogeneity of powerful interest groups. If, for example, some employers insist on retaining an active role in providing health benefits while others are equally ready to abandon this role, a hybrid program can be designed to make both options feasible (although this raises some challenges for administering the program). Hybrid programs reduce the ideological stakes associated with health care reform. Rather than setting the country on an irrevocable course that massively expands or contracts government's role in American society, a competitive hybrid allows strong partisans on both sides of the political fence to envision legacies compatible with their ideological predispositions. Equally important, hybrid programs are arguably less vulnerable to fear campaigns launched by opponents of reform. The specter of "big government" or "greedy insurance executives" loses much of its bite when Americans have the option to choose between public and private coverage.

Competitive Hybrids Are Less Vulnerable to Competitive Politics

A competitive hybrid design is most likely to enhance the prospects for program enactment in eras of divided government and balanced partisanship among the electorate. This was illustrated in the creation of S-CHIP in the mid-1990s. The program's design allowed states to establish coverage either by expanding their existing Medicaid programs (a government insurance option), by subsidizing the purchase of private health insurance, or by combining the two approaches. Arguably, this design was essential for the legislation to pass in the political circumstances of the time.

A public-private hybrid may be most appealing when policy makers are uncertain about how to appropriately design or implement a new initiative. Benefits administered under private auspices take markedly different forms from those provided through the public sector.

The Respective Advantages of Private and Public Benefits

On one hand, private benefits tend to be more adaptable over time and less constrained by political institutions that otherwise inhibit social policy change. Privately administered benefits evidence greater variability in how individuals are judged eligible and how benefits are allocated among the eligible population. Private benefits also tend to be less redistributive in financial impact and may even be regressive in their incidence.

On the other hand, publicly administered programs have been more innovative on the payment side, developing new prospective payment systems for hospitals, physicians, and long-term care facilities. This appears to reflect a public-sector advantage in developing and diffusing innovations that involve substantial economies of scale. Either component of the program may thus demonstrate the feasibility of innovative practices, thereby generating political pressures to extend successful innovations to other components and improving the overall performance of the program.

As a result of these predictable differences in the dynamic properties of public and private benefits, there is potential for learning between the two components of the program. This holds considerable appeal when policy makers worry about affordability of benefits, equitable allocation of resources, or effectiveness in meeting the needs of individual beneficiaries. Arguably, all three of these concerns are evident in contemporary American health policy.

Increased Program Viability

The enhanced capacity for learning across program components can also improve the performance of a hybrid program over time and thus enhance its long-term political viability. Competitive hybrids arguably have several additional advantages over programs that rely exclusively on either public or private insurance.

First, hybrid programs can more readily accommodate regional variation in population density, health needs, or health care resources. To the extent that private insurance yields the best outcomes when there is effective competition among health plans, these performance advantages will typically be limited to metropolitan areas. The public insurance option introduces choice in areas in which private insurance competition would be difficult or impossible to sustain.

Second, a competitive hybrid can more effectively satisfy the preferences of a heterogeneous population. Privatized arrangements typically offer greater flexibility of practice at the cost of reduced stability and consistency. Individuals differ markedly in their willingness and ability to deal with more flexible, but less stable, health insurance arrangements. When some beneficiaries (e.g., those who are most vulnerable) demand substantially more stable, consistent, and secure arrangements, the public components of a hybrid program can better satisfy these preferences. Citizens who feel most at risk of discrimination or other abuses of private discretion will be more supportive of publicly administered benefits.

Hybrid Programs Are Adjustable to Many Political Situations

Third, programs that rely exclusively on public or private administration are often politically vulnerable in eras in which there are frequent changes in party control over Congress or the presidency or frequent shifts in the balance of power between the legislature and the executive branch during periods of divided government. By contrast, hybrid programs can retain their political legitimacy by expanding the scope of either their public or private component to reflect the shifting balance of power or shifting ideological fashions among political elites. Admittedly, expanding a hybrid form of Medicare is not as conceptually elegant or ideologically pure as the grand visions of policy partisans on either side of the ideological spectrum. That is exactly why we believe that expanding Medicare is the most promising approach to breaking the current stalemate. . . . Ultimately, the stakes are too high to continue to debate Medicare reform without also discussing the millions of Americans who lack even basic health security.

> *"It is up to individuals to make the most essential change of all: to accept that early retirement was an historical aberration and to prepare for longer working lives."*

Encouraging Delayed Retirement Will Minimize Age-Related Economic Problems

The Economist

The following viewpoint looks at retirement from an international perspective and argues for abolition of the "traditional" retirement age on the grounds that it has been standard for less than a century and is no longer practical in a world of increased longevity. If the practice of retiring (or requiring retirement) at sixty-five continues, the author asserts, the likely consequence will be a serious drain on the world economy. The Economist is a weekly periodical, published in London.

The Economist, "65 Not Out," vol. 377, no. 8454, November 26, 2005, p. 16. Republished with permission of The Economist Newspaper Group, conveyed through Copyright Clearance Center, Inc.

As you read, consider the following questions:

1. What countries first initiated the practice of retirement at age sixty-five, according to the viewpoint? When?
2. According to the author, how has a later retirement age affected the workforce in New Zealand?
3. How does the author respond to the argument that older workers are mentally and physically less capable than their younger colleagues?

At last the game is opening up. In Germany, the coalition government led by Angela Merkel, the new chancellor, will raise the state-pension age to 67 by 2035. In Britain, the government-appointed Pensions Commission will recommend a similar reform when it reports on November 30th [2005]. Indeed, it will go further and propose that after reaching 67 the state-pension age should keep rising in line with life expectancy.

The reforms are, to say the least, overdue. A retirement age of 65 was first set in Britain in 1925. In Germany it dates back to 1916, when the age of 70 fixed by [Otto von] Bismarck was reduced to 65. This made sense when people could expect to live only a few years after reaching 65. It doesn't now that, happily, they can look forward to a further 20 or more years.

What's more, effective-retirement ages—when people on average stop working—are generally lower than state-pension ages. In many rich countries workers are leaving the labour force closer to 60 than 65, the usual official age. That means fewer people producing and paying taxes and more claiming benefits of various sorts.

Mass Retirement Could Seriously Hurt Public Finances

With the first of the post-war generation of baby-boomers turning 60 next year [2006], the burden of greying populations is no longer a distant threat. Economic growth will slow in rich countries as their labour forces contract. Public finances will be hammered by the soaring ratio of retirees to workers. The finest minds are wrestling with various combinations of public and private savings and insurance schemes, only to find that the circle is unsquarable. It is not pensions that need fixing so much as the workplace.

Later retirement is the answer, but how can it be brought about? Raising the state-pension age helps a lot. New Zealand, for example, pushed it up from 60 to 65 over a nine-year period starting in 1992. As a result, the labour-force participation rates of New Zealanders in their early 60s jumped from 33% to 64% for men and from 16% to 42% for women.

But it is also clear that lifting the pension age is only part of the solution. As a recent report from the OECD [Organisation for Economic Co-operation and Development] suggested, governments, employers and individuals must all change their ways if longer life is to be matched by longer work.

Retiring Young Is Neither an Obligation nor a Right

Governments must revamp not just pensions but also other benefits to make sure that they are not encouraging people to leave the workforce prematurely. Early-retirement schemes, designed to help young people into work, were based on the "lump-of-labour" fallacy, the idea that there is only a fixed amount of jobs to go around. These must go. And in Britain and some Nordic countries, the priority must be to stop incapacity benefits from being misused.

Employers also have much to do. Too many firms still judge workers by their age rather than their performance. They do this not just when they hire and fire but also when they choose whom to train. There is some evidence that older workers are less sharp than younger ones, but experience can

The Historical Roots of Retirement

Retirement has only briefly—and lately—been the status quo. At its core, the institution of retirement was founded on the twin beliefs that the older members of society must be removed from the workforce to make room for the young, and that aging itself was a disability that rendered older people incapable of working to support themselves. Each prong of the argument squarely pointed retirees out of the mainstream of society, into a state of relative isolation.

By contrast, throughout most of history, our ancestors worked until they were physically unable to do so any longer. Elders were an essential part of everyday life, a link between generations, passing on history, tradition, and life skills. . . .

[But by] the late 1800s, [a newly reform-minded and industrialized] society increasingly defined them as a *problem*. People tried to hide the appearance of being old, concealing such physical manifestations as graying hair or false teeth. Physicians advised elders to "lead an absolutely quiet and uneventful life." Dr. William Osler, a prominent physician of the time, even suggested it would be an "incalculable benefit . . . in commercial, political and professional life if, as a matter of course, men stopped work at *that* age." That age was 60.

The concept of retirement was born. It was designed to rid society of the burden of the old, albeit in a socially responsible, benevolent manner. In so doing, society could make room for its young, valuable members in the modern age.

Maddy Dychtwald,
Cycles: How We Will Live, Work, and Buy,
New York: Free Press, 2003.

compensate for the loss of some cognitive abilities, and waning physical strength matters less as economies shift from manufacturing to services.

But it is up to individuals to make the most essential change of all: to accept that early retirement was an historical aberration and to prepare for longer working lives. Their priority must be to remain employable. This will mean a greater willingness to invest in themselves, ensuring that they keep their expertise and skills up to scratch. It will also often mean accepting lower wages if their productivity does decline.

Later Retirement Will Be Beneficial to All

Such reforms may appear difficult, but they will be going with the grain of market pressures and generational change. As younger workers become scarcer companies will become keener on older people. Current age markers will appear increasingly obsolete. Future generations of 50- and 60-year-olds will be better educated and healthier than today's.

The gain from delaying retirement is a prize worth having. And raising employment rates for people in their 50s and 60s will pay a double dividend because this age group is swelling as the baby-boomers mature. Later retirement will boost labour-force growth and ease the strain on public finances.

The reforms to the state-pension age are a promising sign that governments are starting to get serious about their ageing populations. They do not go far enough, given the likely rises in life expectancy over the next 30 years. Yet they still represent a breakthrough in a game that politics has kept static for so long. Now for a drive to the boundary.

> "A 2005 CBS News/New York Times
> national survey found that respondents
> overwhelmingly rejected (77%) the no-
> tion of raising the Social Security re-
> tirement age."

Encouraging Delayed Retirement Is Not Practical

James H. Schulz and Robert H. Binstock

With longevity and the retirement-age population increasing, many commentators say older workers should retain their jobs indefinitely. In this viewpoint, James Schulz and Robert Binstock, both former presidents of the Gerontological Society of America, argue that the idea of delayed retirement is impractical on a large scale. They claim that most retirees have reasons besides job shortages for not working. They also counter the argument that hiring older workers is the only alternative to labor shortages. Schulz is professor emeritus of economics at Brandeis University; Binstock is professor of aging, health, and society at Case Western Reserve University and has directed a White House Task Force on aging.

James H. Schulz and Robert H. Binstock, "To Work or Not to Work: That Is the Question," *Aging Nation: The Economics and Politics of Growing Older in America*, Westport, CT: Praeger, 2006, pp. 137, 138 151–155, 170. Copyright © 2006 by James H. Schulz and Robert H. Binstock. All rights reserved. Reproduced by permission of Greenwood Publishing Group, Inc., Westport, CT.

As you read, consider the following questions:

1. As cited by the authors, what common arguments are offered in favor of older persons' delaying retirement?

2. Schulz and Binstock cite a list of reasons unemployed retirees give for not working. What two responses were more common than that there is no work available?

3. According to Schulz and Binstock, what are some options employers may use instead of hiring older workers?

Increasingly, the "answer" given to population aging and rising pension costs is encouraging or penalizing older people so that they work longer. Many people argue that government and employers must make sure policies and practices do not encourage people to leave the workforce "prematurely." And it is taken for granted that the age of eligibility for public and private pensions must increase. And employers are expected to hire additional older workers.

Such prescriptions, however, contrast sharply with past declining retirement ages and past and current employer practices of getting rid of older workers as early as possible. Workers were liberated in the twentieth century from long years of employment—often years of drudgery. But now the boomers are being told that policies encouraging retirement at an early age must change. Instead, "old folks" should continue working (or go back to work).

The Economist magazine [of November 2005] editorializes that "it is up to [future] individuals to make the most essential change of all: to accept that early retirement was an historical aberration and to prepare for longer working lives. Their priority must be to remain employable. This will mean a greater willingness to invest in themselves, ensuring that they keep their expertise and skills up to scratch. It will also often mean accepting lower wages if their productivity does decline." . . .

There are now increasing numbers of policymakers arguing that, whether we like it or not, the economics of "population aging" *requires* (that is, necessitates) that people work longer in the future.

"Let's Put the Old Folks Back to Work"

Yes, there are some in the United States who have a very clear notion what our reaction to the past changes in labor force participation should be. Given sharply increasing pension costs and the fact that the proportion of younger workers is declining, they argue that older persons should work longer. They point out that most individuals are still relatively healthy and living longer. Moreover, given forecasts of manpower shortages, they predict that older workers who are willing to stay in the work force longer will find it easier to find work.

These two seemingly obvious conclusions about the future, however, turn out to be suspect. It does not necessarily follow from what we know about past work/hiring practices and current attitudes that more "elder work" is the answer. The fact is that most employers may not need, or be inclined to hire, older workers. Moreover, older people may not want the new jobs, even if they are offered. Finally, it is not at all certain that the predictions of labor shortages are correct. Let us look more closely at each of these issues.

First, is it feasible politically to keep the boomers working longer? It is not likely that we can moderate business cycles and keep unemployment low over the long run. Nor will we be able to stop the continuous job destruction that results from shifting manpower needs—given changes in domestic and international markets. Therefore, it would not be surprising if the strong antiwork attitudes of employers, unions, politicians, and workers toward older workers continue.

It is quite likely, in our opinion, that there will continue to be significant support for institutional mechanisms that encourage older workers to retire at early ages. This will be espe-

Many Want to Retire, But Cannot Afford It

The triple whammy of the housing bust, the weakening economy and the turbulent stock market affects most Americans, but few are as shaken as leading-edge baby boomers on the brink of retirement. "There's a lot of sheer panic out there," says financial planner Bert Whitehead of Cambridge Advisors. For many boomers who'd planned the stereotypical retirement play of selling their house and downsizing to a sun-belt condo, falling home values and a lack of offers have put those plans on hold.

Daniel McGinn and Temma Ehrenfeld, "Retirement Postponed," Newsweek, March 31, 2008. www.newsweek.com.

cially true during periods when unemployment is high and/or industries are in decline as demand shifts elsewhere (think about the 2006 situation of GM [General Motors] and Ford [when reduced sales led to massive layoffs]).

The traditional Social Security normal retirement age of 65 is slowly being increased and will be age 67 for those born in 1960 or later. One of the most common recommendations made to reduce Social Security costs is to *speed-up* the increase in the normal age or raise it even further (some have suggested to age 70). Politically, however, this may be hard to do. A 2005 CBS News/*New York Times* national survey found that respondents overwhelmingly rejected (77%) the notion of raising the Social Security retirement age. . . .

Attitude Problems

Without a doubt, the most serious barrier to the reemployment of older workers today is the attitudes of the workers themselves and their potential employers—especially employers' negative attitudes with regard to older worker productivity and the training of older workers. Conventional notions about workers' abilities die hard. Many older workers and most employers truly believe that productivity almost always declines with age and, as the old saying goes, "old dogs cannot learn new tricks."

It is true that as workers grow older many become more choosy about the type of training and work they are willing to do—especially if retirement is a financially feasible option through pension benefits. Also, with increasing age comes an understandable reluctance to uproot oneself and family to make the geographic move often associated with attractive new employment opportunities.

That is in part why survey after survey finds large numbers of "retired" and soon to retire older persons expressing a desire to work, while the reality is that few of them ever do. As the former Commissioner of the Bureau of Labor Statistics, Katharine G. Abraham, observes [in 2004] "many more people express an interest in working at older ages than, in fact, end up doing so. For example, in the first wave of the [National Institute on Aging's] Health and Retirement Study, 73 percent of workers aged from 51 to 61 said that they would like to continue paid work following retirement. . . . Yet, actual employment rates among older Americans are far lower than one might expect from [such] survey responses." Why?

A Variety of Reasons for Not Working

An early [1974] Harris survey focused on "the myth and reality of aging in America." One of the most widely publicized findings from that survey was that a very large number of older persons wanted employment. Not reported were the reasons why they were not working. For only a small minority (15%) was the unavailability of jobs the main reason. When asked, "What keeps you from working?"—the other answers were:

- Poor health (57%)

- "Too old" (28%)

- No work available; a lack of job opportunities (15%)

- Lack of transportation (10%)

- Other reasons (8%)

- Would lose pension benefits or pay too much in taxes if worked (4%)

In 2003, the U.S. Bureau of Labor Statistics similarly asked workers who expressed an interest in working why they were not looking. About one-third reported that they were too discouraged about job prospects. Others cited ill health (10%), family responsibilities (8%), and a variety of other reasons (for example, transportation problems). . . .

You will constantly read that faced with the changing labor force reality, workers and employers *have* to change. However, it seems to us that this may be wishful thinking. The outcome is not as predictable as some would suggest, at least not in the near term.

To begin with, as Peter Cappelli of the Wharton School of Management points out, during the next couple of decades "not only will the [American] population continue to grow, but so will the labor force. The Bureau of Labor Statistics estimates, for example, that the labor force will grow from 153 million in 2000 to 159 million in 2010. The assertion that the labor force will be smaller in the years ahead is simply wrong."

Employers Have Many Options

Moreover, hiring additional older workers is not the only option available to employers who need more labor. Firms can respond to demographic changes in the availability of labor in a number of ways; recruiting and hiring different types of workers (such as older workers) is only one of many ways. For example, throughout the history of industrialized nations, many firms have invested heavily in more physical capital—building or buying machines that substitute for people. Alternatively, employers can encourage government liberalization of immigration policies favoring applicants with needed skills (or, as is common, use undocumented workers). Or, alternately, they can encourage more women with children to stay in the labor force by, for example, offering better day care options. . . .

Some today, in the name of fiscal responsibility, would like to roll back our prior gains in retirement leisure time and make many people work longer. They call it a pension revenue crisis and demand immediate action. Even if the crisis were real (and that is debatable), we have argued that it is unlikely that workers would be willing to solve it by significantly decreasing the retirement/leisure period. Moreover, employers may not change their inherent wariness of older workers, given the various alternatives available. Time will tell.

Periodical Bibliography

The following articles have been selected to supplement the diverse views presented in this chapter.

Ricardo Alonso-Zaldivar	"The Politics of Social Security, Medicare; A New Report Sees Big Trouble. But the Presidential Candidates Aren't Talking," *Los Angeles Times*, March 26, 2008.
Martin Crutsinger	"Trustees Have Bad News for Boomers: Social Security, Medicare Will Soon Be Paying Out More than They Collect," *Houston Chronicle*, March 26, 2008.
Christian Duffin	"Health Care Is Still Age-Biased," *Nursing Older People*, April 2008.
The Futurist	"Retiring Retirement," March/April 2008.
Bridget M. Kuehn	"No End in Sight to Nursing Shortage," *JAMA: Journal of the American Medical Association*, October 10, 2007.
Jennifer Levitz	"Americans Delay Retirement as Housing, Stocks Swoon; Nest Eggs Shrink, Deferring Dreams; 'Freaked Out' Elite," *Wall Street Journal (Eastern Edition)*, April 1, 2008.
Eileen Alt Powell	"As the Oldest Baby Boomers Start Reaching 62, Their Desire to Stop Working Beckons, But Cashing in Early Can Have Pitfalls: 62 a 'Magic' Number for Retirement?" *Houston Chronicle*, March 17, 2008.
Michael Salter and Chris Bryden	"A Question of Ageism," *Pulse*, April 23, 2008.
Allan Sloan	"Social Insecurity, Sooner than You Think," *Washington Post*, March 18, 2008.
Zhang Xueying	"Who Takes Care of Grandmas and Grandpas?" *China Today*, November 2007.

OPPOSING
VIEWPOINTS®
SERIES

CHAPTER 3

What Social Implications Does an Aging Population Present?

Chapter Preface

When people lived in tribes, it was the responsibility of the entire community to support those who were too old to work or to care for themselves. Even after villages and cities predominated, it was long taken for granted that aging citizens would be supported by their grown children or other members of their extended family.

Not until the late nineteenth century did the idea exist that "those who are disabled from work by age or invalidity have a well-grounded claim to care from the state," as Kaiser Wilhelm I of Germany put it in 1881. Eight years later, his government implemented the first recorded social insurance program for retirees. The rest of the world would soon follow.

Perhaps the often taken-for-granted U.S. Social Security system, fostering the idea that government will care for the elderly, is partly responsible for the fact that 1.6 million older Americans—over 6.5 percent of people over seventy—now live in nursing homes. Market research firm Claritas projects that by the year 2020 there will be some 13 million people incapable of completely caring for their own basic needs, many of whom will be living, if not in full-care nursing homes then at least in assisted-living, continuing-care, or independent-living communities.

The availability of so many options for seniors may indicate a growing public awareness that the elder population is a generation of independent-minded seniors who want the freedom to continue making their own choices, rather than letting the government or relatives decide what is good for them. The AARP (the American Association of Retired Persons) reports that 40 percent of Americans over fifty plan to keep working past age sixty-five, and another 20 percent would do so if they felt the additional income was necessary. Thousands of others start their own businesses or become active in volunteer, missions, or charity work. In fact, many volunteer-dependent organizations look to the growing retired population for potential recruits.

Not only are members of the elder generation interested in volunteering and working past retirement age, they also are concerned with enjoying their later years by traveling and participating in other enjoyable pursuits. This behavior sometimes causes conflict among younger people who feel that able-bodied seniors should continue to work if they are able to. They feel it is unfair that active seniors draw Social Security benefits that the working population must fund. The baby boomers—those born between 1946 and 1964—have been called the most selfish generation in American history. Brought up when times were relatively good and when parents who had survived the Great Depression and World War II wanted better for their children, many boomers developed an attitude of entitlement. "These spoilees are as selfish in near-death as they were throughout their lives," writes attorney and political commentator Debbie Schlussel.

> Dow Jones reports that, even though many Boomers are multi-millionaires, they are leaving little of it to their kids and spending it all on themselves before they die. . . . [And] while holding $1.9 million in assets at retirement would seem to assure very comfortable leisure years, paying for that leisure could mean little wealth is left at the end. In fact, more than half (52 percent) of [an American Express] study's respondents reported worrying about running out of money before death.

This chapter will explore the potential implications for society as the boomers move into their sixties and beyond.

> "The retirement decisions made by Baby Boomers . . . could have significant consequences for the nation's social insurance programs, our economy, and their own financial security and quality of life."

Mass Retirements and Corresponding Economic Problems May Be Inevitable

Kathy Krepcio

In the following viewpoint, Kathy Krepcio examines the imminent changes and problems in the workforce as the baby boomers approach retirement age. She concludes that although many boomers will in fact remain in the workforce longer than their predecessors, the danger of economic strain is real, and the country cannot afford an apathetic attitude. She also maintains that the needs of older workers should not be ignored when the resources they counted on prove inadequate. Krepcio is executive director of the John J. Heldrich Center for Workforce Development.

Kathy Krepcio, "Baby Boomers in Retirement: Implications for the Workforce," *Journal of Jewish Communal Service*, vol. 82, no. 3, Summer 2007, pp. 155–158. Reproduced by permission.

As you read, consider the following questions:

1. According to Krepcio, what are the most common arguments supporting the view that the American workforce is not shrinking significantly in the immediate future?

2. As cited in the viewpoint, who said, "Older Americans have contributed much . . . and . . . we owe them . . . the opportunity to continue working as long as they desire"?

3. Whom does Krepcio refer to as the "third group" of older Americans?

A fundamental agent of change said to be shaping the world today is age—or more specifically, our aging Baby Boom generation [Americans born between 1946 and 1964]. Every hour, 330 Boomers turn 60 in this country; 5.5 Boomers age per minute. What does this mean and why should we care?

It means that the retirement decisions made by Baby Boomers—who number more than 78 million in the United States—could have significant consequences for the nation's social insurance programs, our economy, and their own financial security and quality of life. The implications could be enormous.

There Are Not Enough Younger Workers

For instance, if we are depending on younger workers to take up the slack to support older workers' retirement benefits, here are the sobering facts. In 1960, five workers supported every Social Security beneficiary. Today, there are only three. By the year 2031, when all Boomers will be over age 65, there will only be 2.1.

If we are depending on younger workers to fill Boomers' jobs, think again. The retirement of the Baby Boomers is likely to reduce labor force growth. The U.S. Bureau of Labor Statistics projects that the number of people in the prime labor force aged 25–54 will decrease—and continue to decrease—for the next two decades. Boomer labor shortages are already threatening crucial business sectors—such as the energy and aerospace industry, education, and health care—and these sectors are scrambling to come up with solutions to attract, interest, and educate younger workers.

Many Companies Can No Longer Afford Pensions

And, if we are depending on employers to continue to support our health and pension needs, here are today's realities. With concerns about rising costs and eroding American competitiveness, American companies are rethinking their obligation to fund workers' pension and health care plans. Consider some sample headlines from the past few years:

- *United Gets Approval to Shift Pension Plans*

- *General Motors to Freeze Pension Plan for Salaried Workers*

- *After Verizon, Are Pension Freezes on the Way? Other Telecommunications Companies Could Follow Verizon's Lead to Cut Costs*

Not Everyone Expects a Major Labor Shortage

Yet, there are people who believe the doom-and-gloom implications of an aging workforce and retiring Boomers are unfounded. For instance, just recently, America hit the 30 million population milestone, in part because of that other significant demographic factor—immigration. And immigrants who are entering and settling in the United States today are predominantly younger, have a higher birth rate, and have a high labor force attachment rate. Thanks to immigration, predicted labor shortages may not be realized.

In addition, the average American has never had a greater quality of life—both financially and health-wise. The longevity gains in the past century have been made possible by huge advances in medicine and changes in personal behavior. Learning from the example of Eubie Blake, the jazz musician, who said at the age of 98, "If I'd have known I'd live this long, I would have taken better care of myself," Americans are living healthier, longer lives. And more wealth is being created now than at any time in the world's history.

Will the Boomers Keep Working?

The influence of the Boomers has been, and will likely continue to be, enormous. They are the largest segment of our society—making up more than 40% of today's workforce—and they are beginning to gray. What are likely to be their retirement decisions, and in what ways will they shape the future labor market?

Fundamentally, it all comes down to whether they will work longer. Recent economic, social, and demographic trends suggest that the Boomers may work longer than previous generations. And government officials—from the U.S. Federal Reserve Board to the European Commission—want them to do so. What do we know about the factors that will most likely shape their retirement decisions?

Potential Reasons for Delayed Retirements

First, we know that improved health and fewer jobs that are physically demanding may enable more older people to work today than in the past. The ten fastest-growing occupations are predominantly service oriented, reflecting our shift from a manufacturing powerhouse to an economy dependent on knowledge and innovation.

Second, recent Social Security changes may influence retirement decisions for Americans. The removal of the retirement earnings test that allows Social Security retirees at full retirement age to earn income, and the increase in the age at which one can draw down full benefits may affect Boomers' decisions about whether they should keep working.

Reduced Savings and Pensions

Third, low levels of savings—demonstrated by the alarming decline in the personal savings rate to less than zero—may mean that older workers simply cannot afford to stop working. America now has the lowest overall savings rate of any major industrialized nation.

Fourth, changes in and the erosion of employer-provided pension and health insurance may also be a big factor in an individual's choice to keep working. More and more businesses are shedding pensions and pensioners' health care obligations, and the rate of corporate pension plan defaults is rising.

Finally, personal preferences will play a role in retirement decisions. Most people like to work and may simply prefer to keep working. Our own [John J.] Heldrich Center [for Workforce Development] survey on retirement and work suggests that today's working adults not only want to continue working, but are expecting a work-filled retirement. And a 2004 AARP [American Association of Retired Persons] survey reports that 79% of Baby Boomers say they will work at least part time after they turn 65.

The Outlook for Older Workers Seems Positive

In many ways, the outlook for older Americans needing to, or wanting to, continue working seems very positive. [Former President] Bill Clinton once said:

> Older Americans have contributed much to the life of our nation, and to the extraordinary growth and prosperity we enjoy today. We owe them our respect and gratitude; we also owe them the opportunity to continue working as long as they desire.

Now that President Clinton has, himself, become an "older worker," his words ring even truer. Older Americans are in a sense getting younger every day, and many want the option that should be afforded to all Americans of any age—to work and earn. Yet, we also know that older Americans who continue working face significant challenges. Can the Boomers who expect to work do so on their own terms? Although today's 65 may be yesterday's 50, there are several reasons why aging Boomers cannot work or be able to work on their own terms.

The Difficulties for Older Workers

- Some older workers are challenged by physical disabilities or age-related infirmities that limit their ability to remain in or return to the workforce.

- Some may not understand the range of talents they possess that would be valuable in the modern workplace, and some may lack the skills needed to meet the demands of the current and future job market.

- Some may be fearful of a return to a working life they had left to raise children.

- Some need a more flexible work environment and different quality of work (such as part-time work), which many employers are not willing to consider without a significant business case for doing so.

- Finally, others may face real age discrimination in applying for available jobs or have serious difficulty obtaining work that pays a living wage.

Retirement as a New Chapter in Life

Will the new retirement be no retirement? . . .

Many older Americans—those with resources, both financial and social—can expect to view retirement as a new chapter in their life, as a period of reinvention and rejuvenation. This is fundamentally because they are healthier, they do not feel old, and they are optimistic about enjoying another 20 to 30 years of post-career activities. These are people with choices and options, and more likely than not, they will actively choose to remain in the labor market somehow. Work for them will probably be part time—mostly because they want to keep their hand "in the game," they want to bring in a little money, and they want to feel relevant. If they work, it will be on their own terms.

The other older America—people for whom the three-legged stool of retirement is a bit shaky—will not have the resources necessary to enter into "traditional" retirement. These are people who have been working and working hard, but perhaps they have a lower wage job or have been in and out of the labor market during their adult life. Maybe they have a high-school education or less or even some college or vocational training. They may have limited English. They might have no pension plan, or lost a plan, or have a 401(k) that is not likely to earn what they would need to retire. They are more likely to have been in jobs that offered little to no health benefits. And they probably live paycheck to paycheck with little to no savings. For them, a work-filled retirement will be a necessity at best, and perhaps a hardship.

The Third Group of Older Americans

There is, however, a third group: the growing number of older Americans who thought they had resources in place. This is the group that JVS [Jewish Vocational Service] of MetroWest's Maturity Works [job placement for the middle-aged] program is seeing as part of its clientele.

These are people who have worked hard in a full-time job or been in the labor market more often than not. Perhaps they have been running a small business. They have a network of working friends and co-workers. They are educated—maybe even have one or more advanced degrees. Perhaps they have been contributing to a pension plan. They may have some personal savings and assets, such as a car and house. They also may have health benefits and were looking forward to the prospect of collecting Social Security—more likely earlier at 62—to help supplement their savings and anticipated pension benefits.

But this group has been adversely affected by the decline in manufacturing, the growth of corporate reorganizations and alternative work arrangements, and the realities of layoffs and job loss.

Secure Retirement May Be a Myth

For these older Americans, age works against them as a job seeker, as evidenced by the longer time it takes them to find a new job and the wage loss they experience when they find work. For this group, a work-filled retirement may be a reality, but one that is increasingly difficult to find on their terms. And a secure retirement is perhaps a myth.

John F. Kennedy once said, "The Chinese use two brush strokes to write the word 'crisis.' One brush stroke stands for danger; the other for opportunity. In a crisis, be aware of the danger—but recognize the opportunity."

Our aging population is presenting this nation with a crisis that will strain our financial solvency and our future prosperity. At the same time, the effects of global competition are creating economic and workforce changes that are straining our personal standard of living and our financial security—that of future generations.

Time to Act

However, if we want a different reality, if we want to increase options and resources for older Americans, if we want to improve employment opportunities for older workers, and, if we want to ensure that all Americans have real economic security and a decent standard of living as they get older, then we must work together—sooner rather than later—to turn things around. There are, of course, many pressing issues and challenges that need attention. At the Heldrich Center, we believe that one step needs to be taken soon: to address and remediate the widening disconnect between (1) the bewildering global economic scene and the havoc and hardship it is creating on today's disposable worker and (2) current federal workforce policy—most notably, state and national employment and training programs, policies, functions, and activities that are so painfully out of sync with twenty-first-century realities.

Clearly, if we do nothing, a national crisis and more personal hardship will result. Without action, many Americans approaching retirement may be left with little to hang onto but hope.

> "*I can't understand why anybody re-tires. You become expert at what you do, and you make decent money—why stop? To do all the chores that you never wanted to do anyway?*" *(Bob Bennie, MITRE Corporation)*

Mass Retirements and Corresponding Economic Problems Need Not Be Inevitable

Ken Dychtwald, Tamara J. Erickson, and Robert Morison

The following viewpoint argues that massive retirements need not cause serious economic and business problems, especially for individual companies, if employers know ways to attract and re-tain older workers: keeping hiring bias-free, advertising jobs in the right places, and treating older employees with the respect their experience deserves. Ken Dychtwald is founder and chief executive officer of Age Wave and author of a book by that title.

Tamara Erickson is an adviser on implications of the changing workforce; Robert Morison is a leading researcher of business management challenges.

As you read, consider the following questions:

1. What types of job-listing venues do the authors recommend to catch the attention of older workers?
2. According to the authors, when did mandatory retirement first become common in the United States, and why?
3. What five business goals do the authors say can be achieved by providing various work options for the retired?

To safeguard and expand [a] company's talent supply, [the] workforce strategy absolutely *must* include specific plans for employing more mature workers, including those already past the conventional retirement age. Unfortunately, few employers have such plans in place. According to a 2000 survey by the Society for Human Resource Management (SHRM), two-thirds of employers did not actively recruit older workers, over half did not actively attempt to retain key ones, 80 percent offered no special provisions (such as flexible work arrangements) or benefits designed for mature workers, and 60 percent of CEOs [chief executive officers] said their companies do not account for workforce aging in their long-term business plans. . . .

The Principles of Maintaining a Mature Workforce

[Any company that wishes to be the exception must:]

- *First, hire mature workers.* The goal is to recruit mature workers, retain them, and leverage them as lifelong contributors. That means opening new recruiting channels, offering attractive employment deals, and, more fundamentally, rooting out the entrenched age bias in our management systems, human resources practices, and assumptions about people's capabilities.

- *Second, implement flexible retirement.* The goal is to give workers more freedom to remain productive, and employers more freedom to employ them. That means enabling people to adjust their roles and schedules as they approach and pass sixty-five, and expanding options for delaying and forgoing retirement altogether. "Retirement at sixty-five" is a quaint twentieth-century custom, born of economic necessity during the Great Depression—and we must end it out of demographic necessity in the early years of the twenty-first century.

- *Third, advocate reforms in pension and benefits laws.* The goal is to simplify the regulations on pensions, retiree benefits, and working in retirement so that people willingly stay employed. Flexible retirement depends on flexible pension and benefits arrangements, adjustable to mature employees' evolving work patterns and personal needs. But in many countries, including the United States, the Gordian knot [intricate problem] of regulations not only impedes flexible work/flexible retirement arrangements but also motivates employees to retire fully from one company, only to jump to another.

All three involve the realms of social convention and government regulation as well as business operations and performance. Employers can act upon the first two directly. . . .

In 1967, the Age Discrimination in Employment Act (ADEA) banned discrimination against older workers (defined as those over *forty*) in hiring, promotion, retention, training, pay, or benefits. But age bias persists. Corporations operating in the United States might position themselves as unbiased, but their practices suggest otherwise. Advertisers have taken decades to discover the value of pitching everyday products (not just geriatric ones) to older consumers and to depict them as vital rather than senile. Employers must do the same, dropping their assumptions and subtle biases against older workers—and as soon as possible.

Unbiasing Hiring Practices

Hiring processes are generally aimed at younger applicants. Do managers, even young ones, know how to assess the résumé of a sixty-year-old applicant? How would a manager interpret an applicant's twenty-five-year tenure at one company? As a sign of stability and commitment—or inertia and lack of ambition?

Age bias can surface in the wording of a simple job advertisement. "High energy," "fast pace," and "fresh thinking" communicate "youth wanted here," whereas "experience," "knowledge," and "expertise" say "we value maturity." Recruiting channels such as newspaper want ads, "help wanted" signs, or the various job-listing Web sites may not attract older workers. Instead, travel programs for older adults (like Elderhostel), senior centers, country clubs, and retirement communities can all serve as productive recruiting venues. For example, CVS/pharmacy looked at national demographic trends fifteen years ago and concluded that it needed to employ far more older workers. But managers didn't know how to find them—older people shopped in CVS stores but didn't apply for openings. Now the company works through the National Council on the Aging, Experience Works, AARP [American Association of Retired Persons], city agencies, and community organizations to locate productive new employees.

Candidate screening and interviewing techniques can unintentionally put off mature candidates as well. People accustomed to more traditional approaches to demonstrating their skills may balk at having to build something with Legos or explain how M&Ms are made. One major British bank realized that its psychometric and verbal-reasoning tests intimidated older candidates, and so it used role-playing exercises instead to gauge candidates' ability to handle customers. Britain's largest building society, Nationwide, has begun short-listing job candidates through telephone interviews to reduce the number of applicants rejected simply because they look older.

In the past thirteen years, CVS has more than doubled the percentage of employees over age fifty—from 7 percent to 17 percent. It has no mandatory retirement age, so that people can easily join the company at an advanced age and stay indefinitely (six employees are in their nineties); and it boosts its age-friendly image through internal and external publications. Corporate and HR [human resources] department newsletters highlight the productivity and effectiveness of older workers, and CVS teamed with a cosmetics company to produce a maturity-focused magazine, *In Step with Healthy Living*.

Looking at Experience Rather than Age

Older workers can see that CVS honors experience. After accepting a buyout package from his management job at a competing major drugstore chain, fifty-nine-year-old Jim Wing joined CVS as the pharmacy supervisor for the company's southern Ohio stores. Why? "I'm too young to retire," he explains. "CVS is willing to hire older people. They don't look at your age but your experience." Pharmacy technician Jean Penn, age eighty, has worked in the business since 1942. She sold her own small pharmacy to CVS five years ago and began working in another CVS store the next day. She recently received a fifty-year pin (because "they don't make sixty-year pins"). By crediting Penn for time served before she joined the company, CVS loudly communicated how it values experience. Since mature employees often work under much younger managers, CVS fine-tuned its approach to manager training. "You need to train managers whose average age is in the mid-thirties to work effectively with people of all ages. Our experience has

Delayed Retirement Is a Growing Trend

"Sure, there are mornings when I wake up and think, 'It sure would be nice to call in sick,'" [hospital staff services director Joan] Morton said. "But I guess when I turned 65, I found that I just wasn't ready to retire. . . . Plus, I wanted to get myself in a financially more stable place. . . . It's no joke living on a fixed income."

The trend is national: From 2000 to 2006, the proportion of the nation's 65- to 74-year-olds who remained in the labor force increased from nearly one in five to one in four, according to census figures released this week [mid-September 2007].

N.C. Aizenman and Pamela Constable, "Still Working After All These Years," Washington Post, *September 14, 2007.*

helped us identify key issues in managing and motivating older employees," says Stephen Wing of CVS.

Home Depot also has a widespread reputation for hiring midcareer and older employees by hiring dislocated workers—people recently laid off or retired, or those seeking new ways to apply their skills. The company works with senior organizations, community centers across the country, and partners such as the Department of Labor with its One-Stop Referrals program. Home Depot provides flexible schedules, part-time work, flexible vacations, and leaves of absence for various reasons, including once-in-a-lifetime family events or travel opportunities. Team Depot affords many employees the opportunity to "give back to others" through community volunteer projects. As a result, Home Depot enjoys a larger pool of candidates from which to recruit, and the candidates are more qualified. Turnover remains low relative to the retail industry.

Other corporations that routinely hire mature workers include Wal-Mart, where 22 percent of the workforce is fifty-five and older—over a quarter-million employees—in positions ranging from greeter to senior management, most of them frontline with customers. Store managers recruit through senior groups, retiree associations, and church and community groups. Hotel chain Days Inn hires older workers as reservations agents, often part-time and often through a retiree job bank. They experience lower turnover among older workers, and higher customer satisfaction than with younger staff.

The way to succeed in hiring mature workers is simply to get started. As John Rother, AARP's director of policy and strategy, puts it, "What speaks most strongly to the sincerity of the interest in hiring older workers is hiring older workers. If there are other people who have been brought into the company at an older age, that certainly is a powerful message."

Implementing Flexible Retirement

For most of human history, people worked for as long as they could. The first U.S. mandatory retirement law was enacted in 1920—less than one hundred years ago—and covered only employees of the U.S. federal government. Then came the Great Depression, when unemployment reached 25 percent. Desperate to make room for young workers, governments, unions, and employers initiated retirement programs as we know them today, with social security and pension plans. But in doing so, they institutionalized and stigmatized old age. Today, we face a shortage, not a surplus, and so we must phase out "retirement" as we know it.

Most people have heard of "phased retirement"—that is, a staged reduction in work hours and responsibilities ahead of full retirement. For example, Varian, a leading provider of radiotherapy systems, allows employees over fifty-five to negotiate a reduced work schedule if they've served a minimum of five years and plan to retire within the next three. The program addresses employees' requests for flexible and reduced work schedules that ease them into retirement. They typically work four days per week the first year and three days a week thereafter. Half time is the minimum, and two half-timers can job share. Participants retain full medical and dental benefits. Other earnings-based benefits, such as 401 (k) plan contributions and disability and life insurance, are prorated. Participants can request to return full-time if the new schedule creates economic hardship.

Phasing is a variation on the traditional retirement trajectory for employees and, as we noted, a poor one because it eases people *out* of the workforce. We recommend *flexible retirement*, which encompasses flexible roles and work styles, attractive work assignments suited to one's experience and inclination, and reduced hours, flexible schedules, and more control over one's time—*before and after* the point of official "retirement," which loses its significance as flex practices become common.

Active Retirement

Flex retirement means not only *partial retirement*, so that employees can enjoy other pursuits, but also *active retirement*, wherein employees remain productively and socially engaged in the workplace. It means *ongoing work*, often starting before retirement age and continuing decades later, and not shedding employees to reduce costs. Through it, employers can achieve five important business goals, namely to:

1. Retain the services of key employees and top performers who might otherwise join competitors for new responsibilities or reduced hours instead of full retirement.

2. Retain and transfer institutional, industry, project, and customer knowledge and expertise, as flex retirees remain available to train and mentor younger colleagues.

3. Provide highly experienced temporary talent pools and thus moderate fluctuations in staffing needs without tapping traditional temporary agencies or incurring recruiting costs.

4. Retain leadership talent to fill unexpected gaps, facilitate executive transitions, and groom the next generation of leaders for eventual succession. Retirees can act as leaders on demand and help to maintain the leadership pipeline.

5. Control unit cost of labor, getting the same skilled labor at equivalent salary levels but saving on the costs of benefits—not just health care, but pension contributions, vacation time, and others—because these part-time workers are covered by their retiree benefits, which the company is paying for regardless of whether it makes use of the retiree labor.

A Variety of Phased-Retirement Programs

We estimate that only one employer in five offers phased-retirement or retiree-return programs. In a William M. Mercer study, 23 percent of the companies surveyed had formal programs to provide mature workers with flexible work styles. Of these companies, 47 percent offer reduced hours or schedules, 42 percent offer temporary work, 42 percent offer consulting work, 17 percent offer job sharing, 10 percent offer telecommuting, and 45 percent create special positions and assignments, most often involving mentoring, training, or research and development. Moreover, such programs typically lack the scale to affect a corporation's overall staffing, except in organizations like The Aerospace Corporation, where its retiree buffer approaches 10 percent of staff capacity. Most programs function as internal placement agencies for people with sought-after skills and experience. As labor markets tighten, large corporations in other industries should bring these programs up to scale.

Since many pension calculations discourage people from reducing hours or responsibilities prior to retirement, and U.S. government regulations preclude most workers from drawing salary and pension simultaneously from the same employer, many of today's flex retirement arrangements manifest as "retiree return" programs. Typically, the employee takes regular retirement and then returns (after a specified break such as six months) as a contractor, often a maximum of one thousand hours per year. The Internal Revenue Service (IRS) imposes the hourly restriction to discourage companies from substituting full-time employees with retirees, thereby avoiding such expenses as health benefits and Federal Insurance Contributions (FICA). Employees who work more than one thousand hours per year must usually work through an agency and offer their services to other employers as well. Employers with highly variable customer demand or work structured as projects of various length and effort—engineering firms such as The Aerospace Corporation and MITRE as well as professional services firms and companies with seasonal demand such as retailers and tax preparers—can benefit enormously from this contingent workforce.

Retiree Reserves at MITRE Corporation

MITRE Corporation values experience and expertise—the average age of its five thousand employees is forty-six, or about six years above the national average. Seven years ago, it realized that too many people with key knowledge and experience were retiring or leaving to join dot-coms. As a talent retention strategy, it formalized an otherwise ad hoc process for engaging retirees into what it calls Reserves at the Ready. Under the program, any employee with ten years of service can become "part-time on call," working up to one thousand hours per year. They staff projects, mentor younger colleagues, and convey technical expertise and organizational, customer, and project knowledge. Participants are ineligible for paid leave or regular health-care benefits, but almost all have health coverage as retirees. Those receiving pension distribution must wait six months before returning to work. Thereafter, current pension distributions continue, and pension program contributions (to the voluntary unmatched limit) may continue, but retirees cannot initiate new distributions.

On average, one hundred fifty to two hundred people are "at the ready." Because of its long history of engaging retirees as part-time contributors, the company need not advertise the program. But it regularly informs its very active retiree association and the company at large about the program. MITRE also has a part-time work program that some employees use to phase into retirement, assuming a "part-time regular" status and working twenty to thirty hours per week, with benefits. Currently, two hundred fifty to three hundred people (roughly 5 percent of MITRE's workforce) are in the program.

Bill Albright explains the philosophy behind the reserves program: "If you have a culture that doesn't recognize older workers, any retiree work program is going to fail. . . . A lot of organizations believe if you're not in your twenties or thirties, you're a has-been or a cost issue. The corporate culture must value older workers and provide them with working flexibility and learning opportunities, and this must come from top leadership." MITRE received AARP awards in 2001 and 2003 as one of the best places to work for the over-fifty crowd.

Reserve Retirees Speak Out

Ron Coleman, a former systems engineer in MITRE's Economic Decision Analysis Center, is among the reserves. Retiring in 1998 at age sixty-six after nearly ten years of service, he waited a year before signing up for Reserves at the Ready. "I had a lot of stuff to take care of and wanted to get comfortable being retired, and then I felt ready to come back." Since then, he's averaged two projects a year, each four to eight weeks in duration. "I like to golf in the summer, and so am available for work November to March. I can also choose days to go to the office—usually Mondays—and work at home other days—say, Wednesday and Thursday—for a three-day work week. I stay refreshed, keep my hand in, and can train younger people, which I enjoy most."

Bob Bennie is a "serial employee," joining MITRE fresh from graduate school in 1965, then again after stints in academia, retailing, and independent consulting. He kept returning because "it's one of the best companies to work for—great bunch of people and a thoroughly people-oriented organization. MITRE kept offering me the opportunity to learn new things and try new stuff through the years." He's in high demand, essentially working half-time for his old boss, and nears or hits the one thousand-hour maximum each year, working two and a half days a week, half at a local air force base/MITRE office and half at home. "I can't understand why anybody retires. You become expert at what you do, and you make decent money—why stop? To do all the chores that you never wanted to do anyway? I'd rather keep working and pay someone else to do the chores. You spend your career learning how a company works. You're at your peak in terms of knowledge and experience at age sixty or sixty-five. A company should have the foresight to keep you involved and take advantage of the expertise needed."

While most reserves are engineers, any in-demand employee can participate. Theresa Powers joined MITRE as a secretary in 1993 and retired in 2002. She's on call and works when needed, usually a week at a time to replace vacationing secretaries, for a total of about two months a year. She enjoys the arrangement: "I keep my finger in the pot and keep up my skills. The extra money's nice. I see people I like. It's very convenient—just three miles away from my house. And I still have plenty of time to spend with my grandkids." Theresa goes everywhere in the local MITRE facility. "I get to work all over, meet new people, learn new software. And it's good for the company, since I know the systems and am already trained and experienced."

> "The ... older generation [has] ... a
> stronger political voice and politicians
> ... target the greater voting power of
> that ageing group, to the detriment of
> the relatively voiceless young."

An Aging Population Will Be a Financial Burden to Society

Faisal Islam

In the following viewpoint, British journalist Faisal Islam argues that the world's largest age group—those in their fifties and early sixties—will soon be living well in retirement at the expense of people thirty years younger, who already bear the burdens of higher student debt and housing costs than previous generations. Moreover, says the author, many countries are fast becoming "gerontocracies," in which politicians focus primarily on the concerns of their older constituents, the latter not only outnumbering youth but being far more active in politics. Faisal Islam is economics correspondent for the United Kingdom's Channel 4 News.

As you read, consider the following questions:

1. What two age-related German political groups does the author mention?

Faisal Islam, "The Great Generational Robbery," *New Statesman*, vol. 136, no. 4832, March 5, 2007, pp. 34–36. Reproduced by permission.

2. According to the viewpoint, what does the acronym in "SKI-ing" stand for?

3. As discussed in this viewpoint, what do some people refer to as "pig in the pipe?"

Many of you reading this will be thieves. And a good proportion of you will be victims. There is no mugging involved, but a new form of wealth exchange, which economic observers are calling generational robbery: the financial phenomenon whereby one generation—the baby boomers—enjoyed a whole range of economic benefits that are now unattainable to those growing up behind them.

If you are over 50, you will recall a blessed carelessness about money in your twenties and thirties that you probably took for granted at the time. You had free university tuition and, if your parents were sufficiently poor, full university maintenance grants. To that, add free dental care; cheap (relatively) houses with gardens; mutualised building societies; statutory retirement at 65 (probable retirement well before then); and final-salary private pensions. You may be unaware of your complicity, or think it unfair to be blamed for the social and political choices made by others of your generation, but the fact is that the under-35s are facing an unprecedented quadruple whammy: expensive pensions, little chance of getting on the housing ladder, a legacy of student debt and high levels of taxation—a combination of financial burdens and concerns that never clouded the youth of their parents.

The Financial Plight of Today's University Graduate

Consider a 22-year-old graduate. Let's call him Sam. For him, as for his peers, the student debt he left college with was £13,000 [roughly $25,000] (for others today it is closer to £20,000), incurred to repay fees charged at a time when the lifetime payback for having a university degree is decreasing. He is paying for a service that is worth less for him than for the older generation that got it for free and then abolished grants. In addition, the latest wheeze for funding universities is to ask the likes of Sam to donate money to his alma mater. It would be comical to most graduates, were their financial situation not so dire.

With his rent payments, Sam is probably paying off the mortgage of an older landlord who benefited from cheaper house prices. Only a decade ago he would have been four years off becoming a first-time buyer himself; now it is 12 years. Again, his eventual purchase will be a transfer of hundreds of thousands of pounds from young to old. In his tax payments—which will rise by 1.5 per cent of GDP [gross domestic product] or the equivalent of 4p on income tax in his lifetime—he'll be paying the pensions of a golden-aged era of retirees who stood by as similar pensions were closed to him. Not that he will need much of a pension, as he may be working into his seventies anyway.

It Is Very Difficult to Buy a Home Now

If Sam wants to become a homeowner, he'll have to work fast. The first rung of the housing ladder is rapidly disappearing. Indeed, with mortgage terms being extended to 30, 40 or even 50 years, it is questionable whether the ladder exists at all. More of those struggling to buy property today should expect to stay much longer in the first flat they struggled to buy than previous generations. High house prices are not creating wealth—they are merely redistributing it to the old and rich from the young and poor.

Demographics show the root of the problem. On the Office for National Statistics website there is an animation which shows age distribution in Britain. The population pyramids that once showed many young people at the bottom supporting a small number of older people at the top is being flipped on its head. The result is an older generation with a stronger political voice and politicians who target the greater voting power of that ageing group, to the detriment of the relatively voiceless young. At the time of the 2005 election, [research company Ipsos] MORI calculated that the over-55s had 4.2 times the voting power of 18- to 34-year-olds. We are sliding towards a gerontocracy.

Gerontocracies Are Developing in Europe

Other European countries are further down the road. The balance in favour of older voters will make Germany a gerontocracy within seven or eight years, according to the economist Hans-Werner Sinn. The signs are already there. Nuremberg is building swingless playgrounds for senior citizens in their parks and an advocacy group for older people, the Grey Panthers, nearly made it into the Berlin regional parliament in last September's [2006] elections. In response, young Germans have formed the Foundation for the Rights of Future Generations, and will this year try to get the Bundestag [Germany's national parliament] to change the constitution to protect those rights.

In the UK [United Kingdom], the number of people over 40 will overtake the under-forties by 2021. By 2031, the average age of the population will climb from 39 to 44, and over-65s will constitute nearly a quarter of the population, compared to the sixth they comprise now. This is yielding a new age-related politics. Most headway has been made in the part of Britain that is ageing fastest: Scotland. The Scottish Senior Citizens Unity Party already has a presence at Holyrood and is ramping up the number of its candidates for this May's [2007] elections.

Taxes Are Falling for the Old, Rising for the Young

The hand of an ageing population can be seen in certain postwar changes to the British tax system. According to Martin

Entitlement Programs Are a Potential Danger to the Federal Budget

Under 2004 [Social Security] Trustees' intermediate assumptions and CBO's [Congressional Budget Office's] long-term Medicaid estimates, spending for Social Security, Medicare, and Medicaid combined will grow from 8.5 percent of GDP [gross domestic product] today, to 15.6 percent of GDP by 2030—just 25 years from now.

Let's be clear about what this means. By the time today's 40 year-old reaches age 65, our nation will be spending $1 out of every $6.40 produced by the entire economy, just to support these three entitlement programs.

The farther into the future one looks, the larger these programs grow relative to the economy. Today, total spending by the *entire* federal government accounts for about 20 percent of GDP. *Absent significant reform of our entitlement programs, in just 75 years, Social Security, Medicare, and Medicaid alone are projected to consume 25 percent of GDP.* This means that one-quarter of the nation's total output will be spent on these three programs alone.

This is before we have set aside a single penny to support national defense, homeland security, environmental protection, education for our children, or any number of other national priorities. Nor does it include rising expenditures by state and local governments. Furthermore, that is just the consumption that is publicly financed, i.e., that which is to be paid out of taxes on future generations. One must also keep in mind the obvious fact that the workers of tomorrow—who are our children today—will still need money to live on as they start careers, buy homes, raise families and save for their own retirement.

Jeffrey R. Brown,
testimony before the U.S. Senate Committee on the Budget,
February 17, 2005.

Weale, of the National Institute of Economic and Social Research, the amount of tax on wealth—such as housing, which is usually owned by older people—has fallen dramatically since the end of the war [World War II]. Meanwhile, taxes on those who work (normally younger people) have risen steadily. Some pensioners are very poor. Most are not. The greatest proportion of wealthy people in Britain are over 55; 70 per cent of those worth more than half a million pounds are over 55. Wealth statistics in Britain are sketchy, partly because they are derived from data on inheritance. However, the last set of official figures showed that, on average, 55- to 69-year-olds had £109,000 in amassed assets—treble those of 25- to 39-year-olds. Over-55s are the biggest owners and traders of shares.

To some degree, that is to be expected. The older you are, the longer you have had to amass assets. But these figures do illuminate the reality behind those depictions of a poverty-stricken old age. Certainly, there are those who need help. But whereas 27 per cent of pensioners were classified as living in poverty a decade ago, that is now down to 17 per cent.

Rich Middle-Class Pensioners

It is possible, on the one hand, to recognise the very real issue of pensioner poverty, while also pointing out that there are huge numbers of middle-class pensioners who have done tremendously well out of the housing market, for example, and who are now providing rather good custom to [tour operator] Saga and the *QEII* [*Queen Elizabeth II* cruise ship]—"SKI-ing" (Spending the Kids' Inheritance) their way through a golden retirement.

This is the economics of the age we live in, a political time bomb that parties ignore at their peril. David Willetts, the Conservatives' licensed freethinker, has floated the idea of generational tensions replacing class difference. Some Lib Dem activists are debating it, one of them blogging recently:

"Already half of the tax the under-35s pay is being spent on pensions, healthcare and social services for the elderly, and this burden will increase with demographic change. Younger generations are beginning to perceive this as generational theft on a massive scale." Some point out that the money for supporting asset-poor pensioners may be more sensibly found from a wealth tax on cruise-addicted middle-class pensioners, rather than younger workers. Labour supporters, meanwhile, point out that the government has spent more on the younger generation through investment in schools, although single, childless young adults are not the winners in Labour's quiet redistributions.

"The Pig in the Pipe"

The economic impact of this glut of postwar children is familiar to those in the City [London] who refer to it as the "pig in the pipe"—the visible signs of the baby boomers charging through the decade. They embraced social liberalism, flower power and a large state when they were teenagers, and low taxes, a smaller state and loadsamoney individualism in their period of high disposable income. Then, on the realisation of their own mortality, up goes spending on the health service and pensions. Fifty- to 64-year-olds have the largest carbon footprints—20 per cent bigger than other age groups'—although they care the most about climate change, a phenomenon that will not affect them.

Ultimately, as pensioners take the justifiable decision to fight for their rights, it should be no surprise that younger generations do the same. But they have yet to do so in Britain. Weale suggests they may be too busy working, or don't believe in politics. Either way, apathy is costing them. Or is it poetic justice that live-for-today youngsters are losing out to a selfish generation? Perhaps we are seeing the scary sight of a generation that has been rather brutal in getting its own way squeezing everything it can out of its children.

> "Instead of viewing older Americans ex-
> clusively as a drain on society ... they
> should be considered a tremendous as-
> set that can be tapped to help solve so-
> cial problems."

An Aging Population Can Contribute Much to Society

Suzanne Perry and Michael Aft

In the following selection, Suzanne Perry and Michael Aft report that nonprofit organizations and government agencies are providing opportunities for baby boomers to participate in community service. Many volunteer-reliant organizations have been slow to focus on recruiting from the retired population, say the authors, but that is changing with the sixty-five-and-older group expected to double in the next quarter century. Although baby boomers appear less interested in volunteering than the present generation of retirees, the larger size of the boomer population should compensate for that lack of interest and still provide adequate numbers of recruits. Suzanne Perry and Michael Aft are writers for the Chronicle of Philanthropy.

As you read, consider the following questions:

1. According to the authors, how many potential volunteers have signed up for the retiree-focused nonprofit group Peace Corps Encore?

2. What do the authors report as the primary flaws in many charities' "outmoded view of volunteering?"

3. What organization awarded $1.5 million in grants toward the "next generation" of national service programs?

When Chris Klose was 16, he was electrified by President John F. Kennedy's famous appeal: "Ask not what your country can do for you—ask what you can do for your country." In 1968 Mr. Klose followed through and joined the Peace Corps, serving two years in the Punjab region of northwest India helping farmers develop new varieties of wheat.

Mr. Klose later pursued a career in public relations, but he always dreamed of finding a way to reignite the passion he felt as a Peace Corps volunteer. "It was the transformative experience of my life, and I want to give back," says Mr. Klose. "I've been thinking about it for 35 years."

Now, at age 60, Mr. Klose is translating his dream into action. About two years ago, he and a longtime friend with whom he served in the Peace Corps, Jerr Boschee, founded a nonprofit group to recruit former Peace Corps volunteers for short-term overseas assignments.

The group, Peace Corps Encore, has signed up more than 600 potential volunteers, opened an office in Washington [D.C.], and hired an executive director. It has also attracted foundation money—$150,000 from the UPS [United Parcel Service] Foundation, which asked that at least 40 percent of the volunteers be 55 and older, and $25,000 from the W.K. Kellogg Foundation.

Aging Boomers Are an Asset

Mr. Klose and Mr. Boschee are part of a growing effort in nonprofit and government circles to make community service—through paid jobs or volunteer work—a central part of the lives of the baby boomers as they reach their 60s and beyond. Proponents of getting the boomers involved in non-profit activities say they hope to radically reshape the way society thinks about the graying of America. Instead of viewing older Americans exclusively as a drain on society who are going to bankrupt health-care and Social Security programs, they argue, they should be considered a tremendous asset that can be tapped to help solve social problems.

The movement has been percolating for the last decade, but it has exploded in recent months, thanks to the approach of a much-publicized milestone—January 1, 2006, the day the oldest baby boomers start turning 60. And it is likely to gain more momentum next month [December 2005], at the White House Conference on Aging, which will unite 1,200 delegates from across the country to develop recommendations to influence national policy on aging over the next decade.

"Social engagement is crucial to the physical and psychological well-being of elderly citizens," the agenda states. "It is an equally important way in which senior citizens can contribute to their communities."

The Number of Retired Americans Will Double by 2030

The boomers are getting so much attention in part because of the sheer size of the generation—more than 77 million people were born from 1946 to 1964. As they age, they will help double the number of Americans who are 65 and older from about 35 million today to more than 70 million in 2030. They are also better educated than their parents' generation, and have longer life expectancies.

Like Mr. Klose, many Americans who came of age in the 1960s were influenced by President Kennedy's call to service and by the era's social activism, so they are expected to be responsive to appeals from charities.

And charities are likely to need workers more than ever—many of their leaders are themselves baby boomers and are expected to leave their jobs in the coming decade, either to retire or to try new opportunities in business, government, and elsewhere.

But the boomers are a fussy bunch, and charities need to learn how to accommodate them. They want positions where they can make a difference, research shows, and most non-profit groups have not figured out how to offer them those kinds of opportunities, experts say.

Overcoming Hurdles

David Eisner, chief executive of the Corporation for National and Community Service, a federal agency that operates the RSVP [Retired Senior Volunteer Program], Foster Grandparents, and Senior Companion programs for older volunteers, says his group knows "there are some hurdles in the way" when it comes to getting more older people linked with satisfying volunteer jobs. "One of the big ones is cultural, one of the big ones is operational, in the nonprofit sector," he says.

Many charities, he says, have an outmoded view of volunteering, failing to recognize the value of putting people with years of experience in business, the professions, and government to work. "We have nonprofits that are used to thinking about hiring a consultant to develop a strategic plan, then bring the volunteers in to do the clerical work," he says. "No one's flipping it. People haven't figured out how to bring the volunteer in to do the strategic plan, then hire at a lower cost the people to do the clerical work."

A survey of more than 800 leaders and coordinators of volunteers at affiliates of 20 national nonprofit organizations released last spring, confirmed Mr. Eisner's views. While most charity leaders said they valued the potential contribution of older adults, few showed much interest in stepping up efforts to attract and retain them—partly because they were preoccupied with daily operational challenges and money problems.

"Developing strategies to tap the resources of older adults through paid and unpaid positions was beneath the radars of most local nonprofit officials," says the March 2005 executive summary of the survey, which was conducted by the National Council on the Aging.

Sold-Out Events

Even so, signs of change are in the air.

Dick Goldberg, director of Coming of Age, a program in Philadelphia that promotes volunteering and community leadership for people age 50 and older, says that when he organized a conference for nonprofit leaders in April [2005] on "50-Plus Volunteering: the Wave of the Future," 250 people showed up from as far away as Delaware, New Jersey, New York, and Washington, D.C. Since the auditorium only fit 200, some participants had to watch the plenary sessions on a television feed in a separate room.

In October, the program advertised a session with Ellen Freudenheim, an expert on retirement issues, to discuss "why boomers and recent retirees want to find work that makes a difference—and how to do that." A headline on the Coming of Age Web site soon read: "November 14 Boomervision! session is SOLD OUT."

"What we have found with everything we have initiated this past year is there are more people who want to be involved than we have room for," Mr. Goldberg says. . . .

Seeking Models

Several organizations are working on national efforts to highlight projects and practices that can serve as models for other groups—including the National Council on the Aging, in Washington, a network of organizations that operate programs for older people. In 2003 the council started Respect-

Retirees in Volunteer Work

The value of volunteer work in the United States is estimated to be $272 billion, or 2.5 percent of the nation's GDP [gross domestic product], and older Americans provide millions of dollars of equivalent productivity in volunteer activities. Jay Winsten, associate dean of the Harvard School of Public Health and director of the school's center for health communication, said he anticipated that when the baby boom generation begins to retire in 2011 they would expand the volunteer sector in the nation's $10 trillion plus economy beyond almost eighty-four billion hours of volunteer work each year. Florida has passed legislation to support programs that encourage volunteers to contribute services, for which they receive "time currency" or "time dollars" that can be cashed in when the volunteers themselves need services.

Individuals who have retired from the worlds of science, business, and academia, among others, could teach, mentor, and sponsor young people. A registry of retired scientists who want to continue working or to volunteer their services should be kept by the National Academy of Sciences and the Department of Education. They could lead after-school enrichment programs for children, in this nation of science illiteracy. Moreover, we should not lose the great gifts of craftsmanship and the arts carried out by older persons.

Robert N. Butler, The Longevity Revolution:
The Benefits and Challenges of Living a Long Life,
New York: PublicAffairs, 2008.

Ability, a program to help nonprofit groups make better use of older Americans, with a $3.5-million grant from the [multinational] Atlantic Philanthropies.

"Back then, this whole issue of aging, while it was being talked about by various groups, had not really become mainstream," says Tom Endres, director of RespectAbility. "The first impetus was, what can we do to raise awareness and move from a state of awareness to acceptance?" RespectAbility is now on a quest to find examples of organizations that have taken an innovative approach to engaging older adults—and to share their secrets with other charities. It will give awards of $10,000 apiece to 5 or 10 groups that have developed programs to give older adults meaningful roles that benefit others. The group has identified 34 semifinalists and will announce the winners next spring.

Retired Executives as Nonprofit Coaches

One of the semifinalists is the Executive Service Corps of Chicago, which, with a grant from the Retirement Research Foundation, also in Chicago, started a program about three years ago to recruit retired executives to coach executive directors of local nonprofit groups. The organization provides numerous executive services for nonprofit groups, but coaching is now the most-requested one, says Meg Herman, manager of the program.

"It's lonely at the top," she says. Nonprofit leaders "want a strategic thought partner whose interests aren't threatened." The group has about 30 active coaches, many of whom served as top executives at major businesses. Many have also served on nonprofit boards. Coaches get intensive training before they are matched with an executive director.

Only a few have not worked out, she says. Occasionally, a high-powered former executive finds it is difficult to be a "sage on the side" rather than a "star on the stage," she says.

The Next Generation

The Corporation for National and Community Service [based in Washington, D.C.] is also offering incentives to nonprofit groups that develop new ways to engage older volunteers. In

September [2005] it awarded $1.5 million in grants for what it called the "next generation" of national-service programs, including those trying innovative ways to attract baby boomers.

Big Brothers Big Sisters of El Paso [Texas] won $207,500 through the grant program. Beth Senger, the group's chief executive, says the charity is setting up a program to recruit baby boomers to help the organization in new ways. While Big Brothers Big Sisters traditionally recruits young adults to act as "buddies" to children, and older volunteers to serve as mentors in schools, the El Paso affiliate now hopes to attract people who may be looking for something that involves less commitment—for example, auditing financial records or consulting on information technology, with the option of working from home, Ms. Senger says.

"The assumption is that people in this age bracket are professionals in their field, they're at a place in their lives where they've learned a lot," she says. "Why are we dictating to them what we want when they probably have wonderful ideas about how they can help?" . . .

Even a Few Boomers Can Make a Difference

A report on civic engagement and baby boomers published last year [2004] by the Harvard School of Public Health and the MetLife Foundation noted that boomers are less devoted to community service than their parents, or the "Greatest Generation"—they vote less, read newspapers less, and are less apt to join churches or civic organizations—and may need a big push.

But Jay Winsten, co-director of the Harvard/MetLife project on civic engagement, says that even a small percentage of baby boomers could make a big difference. "Although there are 77 million baby boomers, we don't need to attract all of them to civic engagement," he says. Even if only 10 percent of them heeded the call, "it could have an amazing impact."

> "If news about layoffs, foreclosures and
> the wobbly stock market has you trem-
> bling . . . the uncomfortable truth is
> you can never save too much."

Retirement Planning Is Vital

Jeffrey R. Kosnett

*Examining one couple who has half a million dollars in savings
that grows by twenty-seven-thousand dollars a year as an example of frugality, the following viewpoint considers whether it
is possible to overplan for retirement, to save too much? After
considering the drawbacks of sacrificing all present enjoyment in
the name of the future, the rewards of saving, investing, and
spending wisely, and the couple's plans for the coming years, author Jeffrey Kosnett concludes that given the current economic
situation, it is nearly impossible to oversave. Kosnett is a senior
editor of* Kiplinger's Personal Finance, *specializing in investments and financial planning.*

As you read, consider the following questions:

1. As exemplified by the viewpoint's Moore family, what
   are some of the ways in which a family can save money?

Jeffrey R. Kosnett, "Can You Save Too Much for Retirement?" *Kiplinger's Personal Finance*, vol. 61, no. 11, November 2007, p. 26. Reproduced by permission.

2. What actions does financial adviser Jeff Broadhurst recommend to ensure having enough money for retirement?

3. According to Kosnett, how much will the Moores have accumulated in twenty years?

Kerry and Robert Moore defy the popular notion that Americans spend everything they earn and then some. Kerry, 37, an engineering manager for the U.S. government in the Denver area, sets aside 30% of her pay. She directs $597 to the government's 401(k)-style retirement plan every two weeks, $100 a month to each of three mutual funds and $25 monthly to 529 college-savings accounts for sons Max and Sam, ages 5 and 2. Kerry and Robert, 39, also add $4,000 a year each to their Roth IRAs [individual retirement accounts]. All told, the Moores save $27,000 a year and have already accumulated about $500,000. Plus, with 18 years on Uncle Sam's payroll, Kerry is in line for a good pension.

The Moores are in good-enough financial shape that Robert, who used to work at Lockheed Martin and Raytheon, stays home with the kids, while Kerry works full-time and pursues a master's degree. She's also expecting a new baby. Still, Kerry has a nagging feeling that her saving habits are over-the-top. "Am I saving too much?" she asks.

The Trouble with Saving Everything

That's not a flip question. Too much thrift "can be an impediment to a happy lifestyle," says Rebecca Preston, of Preston Financial Planning, in Providence, R.I. She advises well-set clients who are young or approaching retirement to "stop pinching every nickel until the buffalo screams" and to move to a more desirable location, switch to lower-paying but more enjoyable work, or just have a good time.

Jeff Broadhurst, of Broadhurst Financial Advisors in Lansdale, Pa., echoes Preston. He says people who are careful with

Calculating a Retirement Budget

Only 43% of surveyed workers say they and/or their spouse have tried to calculate how much money they will need to live comfortably in retirement, according to the Employee Benefit Research Institute in Washington.

Yes, budgeting is always difficult—and even more so for retirement. (What will utilities cost in 20 years?) But making the effort is an essential step in planning for later life.

Thomas Fair, 60, who runs his own auto business in Rhode Island, says he had no idea how much money he was spending—until his wife all but demanded that they sit down and discuss their finances and future. As it turned out, "the year before last, we spent $8,200 on our [five] dogs and $4,000 on wine," Mr. Fair says. "Now we have a monthly meeting, and she tells me, 'This is what we have in savings, this is what we have in the checkbook.'"

Glenn Ruffenach,
Wall Street Journal (Eastern Edition), *September 22, 2007.*

their finances and have good health benefits and pensions almost always have enough money in the end. Broadhurst also suggests that families with ample savings, good credit records and secure jobs consider taking advantage of softer housing prices to trade up. Kerry, who isn't interested in moving, "sounds like she's asking for permission to spend," Broadhurst says.

A sound investment plan gives the Moores flexibility. Their largest pot, roughly half of the total, is in Kerry's government-sponsored retirement plan. She directs almost 90% of her contributions to a mix of U.S. and overseas index funds and the rest to bond funds. Funds in taxable accounts include T.

Rowe Price Mid-Cap Growth, a fine performer, and the improving Janus Worldwide. In addition, Robert has a pile of Lockheed stock. At their current pace of saving, and assuming a 7% annualized return, the Moores are on track to accumulate $2.5 million to $3.5 million in 20 years, depending on taxes and whether Robert returns to work.

That should help the couple through the school-bill crunch for Max, Sam and 13-year-old Sarah, who aspires to train as a chef. Assuming Robert resumes his career and Kerry earns more promotions, paying for culinary school should be as easy as frying an egg.

So, is Kerry Moore saving too much? Yes, if you don't think the typical family needs millions of dollars for education and a comfortable retirement. No, if news about layoffs, foreclosures and the wobbly stock market has you trembling. If so, the uncomfortable truth is you can never save too much.

> *"Astonishing advances in anti-aging medicine may soon make centenarians as common as July fireflies. ... However, the longer we live, the more money we need."*

Standard Retirement Planning Overlooks Financial Hazards

Cait Murphy, Julia Boorstin, and Margaretta Soehendro

The following viewpoint argues that standard retirement plans of yesteryear may not be sufficient today, given rising prices, reduced interest rates, declining funds for government benefits, and longer life spans. The authors recommend that retirement planning should include a careful choice of investments, an emphasis on healthy lifestyle (to reduce medical expenses), and hedging on the side of longevity when calculating lifelong financial needs. Cait Murphy is an assistant managing editor of Fortune; *Julia Boorstin is a CNBC reporter; and Margaretta Soehendro is managing editor of* AsiaMedia.

As you read, consider the following questions:

1. As cited by the authors, what is "hedonics," and how does it affect the value of today's goods?

2. According to the viewpoint, what have falling interest rates done to the value of Treasury bonds?

3. Why are women at particular risk of not having enough money saved for retirement, as mentioned in the viewpoint?

You've been maxing out your 401(k) since you began working. You piled into stocks through the raging bull market of the '80s and '90s. Your house has quintupled in value. And now you're feeling pretty darn good about how well you'll live in retirement. A little smug, even.

This story is for you. A host of financial planners and other investment pros we consulted warn that even the most diligent savers and savviest investors may face serious threats to their financial health—ones they may not have fully factored into their retirement planning. Here are five of the most significant threats, plus our advice on what you can do to counter them.

1. Lower Stock Returns. It's an article of faith for most investment pros: Over the long term, stocks rise—and they rise faster than bonds or cash. Since 1926, the S&P 500 [an index used to track stock-market activity] has returned an average of 10.4% a year, vs. 5.5% for bonds and 3.7% for cash, according to Ibbotson Associates. Long-term averages, though, obscure the fact that sometimes stocks stink.

Timing matters. If you started in the early '80s, terrific: During the great bull market [in which investors are confident and thus motivated to buy more stocks] of 1982 to 2000, stocks were rising so fast that it almost didn't matter whether you were investing enough. Appreciation made up for it. But if you started in 1999, no such luck. "What is commandingly clear," says Jim Grant, editor of the newsletter *Grant's Interest Rate Observer*, "is what a sweet golden moment [the early 1980s] was for financial assets." Back then, Treasury yields were around 12%, and 12-month trailing price/earnings ratios were in the single digits. Now, conditions have neatly reversed, with low yields and P/E [price-to earnings] ratios [a measure of the price paid for a share relative to the annual income or profit earned per share] averaging 20. So for the foreseeable future, investors will probably be riding the equivalent of a horse-drawn trolley, not a bullet train. At *Fortune*'s recent retirement roundtable, the consensus expectation for stocks was just 6% a year for the next five to ten years.

Does that mean you should be pulling out of stocks? Of course not: Even at that tepid pace, they're still likely to be the best available option. But reduced returns are a compelling argument for saving more money. They are also an argument for paying much more attention to stock-investing costs that you can control, such as fees (by using, for example, a discount broker and low-cost mutual funds) and taxes (by buying and holding when possible rather than by rapidly trading).

2. Inflated Inflation. Inflation is retirees' worst enemy, eating away at the value of their assets and their standard of living. The consumer price index [CPI] rose from an annual average of 2.5% since 1991 to 3.5% in April [2005] before falling slightly. No one thinks the U.S. is about to become 1980s Argentina or Weimar Germany, where hyperinflation devastated society. But as anyone who remembers the 1970s can tell you, inflation here is quite capable of hitting the double digits. Even a small rise in inflation can have devastating effects. A monthly pension of $3,000 will buy only $2,055 worth of goods in ten years, assuming 3.5% inflation. At 4.5% inflation, that number falls to $1,849. At 5.5%, it's $1,665.

What's more, real-life inflation may be much worse than the official statistics indicate. Take a look at the CPI's methodology. Its statisticians make use of "hedonics," a method of attaching a value to the increase in the quality of new goods. Here's an example: If your new computer cost $500 more than your old one but had more than $500 worth of improvements (according to Treasury wonks), the CPI says it actually cost

Look at What *You* Can Do

Six months of aggressive interest-rate cuts by the Federal Reserve may be good for the economy, but it's bad news for many seniors who rely on fixed-income investments. . . .

"You look at what you can control," said Stuart Ritter, certified financial planner with mutual fund giant T. Rowe Price, "You can't control the stock market. You can't control interest rates. What you can control is how much you save, how much you spend and how you invest."

Kathy M. Kristoff, Los Angeles Times, *March 30, 2008.*

less. The sticker price for a car bought in the U.S. has risen 338% since 1979, according to the Leuthold Group, an economic consultancy. But because of hedonic adjustments, the CPI reflects only a 62% rise.

Another curious thing about the CPI is that it does not calculate changes in housing costs by the sales prices. Instead it uses a figure that estimates what homeowners would get if they rented out their homes. In 2004, national housing prices rose more than 11%, but the CPI calculates that they rose about 2%. Bill Gross, founder and managing director of PIMCO, an investment company that has more than $464 billion under management, estimated in late 2004 that real inflation could be a full percentage point higher than the CPI. That means, for example, that Social Security payments, which are linked to the CPI, may lag real-life expenses.

How do you cope with inflation? For one thing, don't shy away from stocks, which tend to outpace it. Treasury inflation-protected securities (TIPS) are low-risk investments that are guaranteed to keep pace with the CPI (although as we noted above, that may not reflect the true cost of living). But the most important thing you can do is to be realistic when developing a financial plan about how much money you'll need to maintain your standard of living in retirement.

3. Piddling Interest Rates. In the '60s, the generation gap was about sex, drugs, and rock & roll. Today it's about interest rates. The Federal funds rate is at 3%, and ten-year T-bills are at 4.1%—not much higher than inflation. That's great for younger people buying homes and taking out loans to fix them up. It's rotten for older ones trying to live off their savings. Just a few years ago a retiree with $1 million to invest could have stashed it all in supersafe Treasury bonds and locked in an interest stream of $64,000 a year. Today that same $1 million would get you only $41,000 a year.

There are no easy ways to cope with lower rates. One remedy, mentioned above, is to sock away more money. Dividend-paying stocks also offer some relief: Many financially strong companies are yielding 3%, 4%, or more. Those payouts are taxed at a lower rate than interest on bonds, and many companies raise dividends over time, while bond payments are fixed. Also, avoid long-term bonds and stick with those that mature in just two to five years, suggests Gary Schatsky, a New York City financial planner. These days, the shorter-term bonds pay almost as much, and if rates do rise, you'll be able to swap them for new bonds with fatter yields when they mature.

4. A Medicare Disaster. President [George W.] Bush's big plans for Social Security have attracted all the headlines lately. But the fate of Social Security should scare retirees far less than the fate of Medicare. In terms of net present value—the amount the government would have to set aside to generate the returns necessary to pay future obligations—Medicare is running $63 trillion short. The comparable figure for Social Security is a mere $8 trillion.

That's the conclusion of recent work by Jagadeesh Gokhale, a senior fellow at the [public policy research foundation] Cato Institute and former economic advisor to the Cleveland Federal Reserve, and Kent Smetters, an economist at Pennsylvania University's Wharton School of Business. Essentially, they added up all the promises the federal government has made regarding Social Security, Medicare, Medicaid, and so on; they also projected nonentitlement expenditures. Then they looked at government revenues and totted up the difference between current and future obligations and projected revenues. Taking into account surpluses in some areas, they came up with a total figure of $66 trillion. Then our dismal scientists asked what the feds would have to do to fill this hole. Answer: Raise the payroll tax for Social Security and Medicare by another 16.6 percentage points (it is 15.3% now) or the income tax by more than two-thirds. Now and forever.

Something's got to give and that something is bound to include generous Medicare coverage. By the time today's working stiffs retire, they will almost certainly be paying more of the cost of health care themselves. So if you haven't already, start embracing a healthier lifestyle pronto. And consider Medigap insurance, which helps cover the difference between what Medicare covers and what you are responsible for paying. For more information on Medigap policies, go to AARP.org/healthcare/medicare.

5. Longer Lives. A generation ago, the typical guy who got his gold watch [upon retiring] at 65 would keel over at 78. Today, a 65-year-old man is far more likely to live to 82. His 65-year-old female counterpart is living longer too: to 85. And astonishing advances in anti-aging medicine may soon make centenarians as common as July fireflies. That's not such great news for retirement plans, however. The longer we live, the more money we need.

Women are at particular risk. Not only do members of the allegedly weaker sex outlive men by several years, but they are at the top of the demographic charts when it comes to reaching really, really old age: Two-thirds of the over-85 set are female. But because women tend to have more fractured work histories—they are twice as likely to work part-time, for example—and to make less money when they do work, their retirement kitties are much thinner. Young women (ages 21 to 34) are also more likely than men to carry debt—something Cindy Hounsell of the Women's Institute for a Secure Retirement (WISER) in Washington calls the "Carrie Bradshaw effect," after the *Sex and the City* character who belatedly realized that she could not monetize her $40,000 worth of Manolo Blahniks [shoes] into a down payment on an apartment.

Then there's divorce, a phenomenon that will likely affect the baby-boomers more than any previous generation. Pension assets are considered the property of both spouses, but not every state requires that they be divided when the marriage breaks up. And of course, an ex-wife has no right to future pension benefits that accrue to her former spouse. That's if the husband has a pension at all: Traditional company-funded pensions are fast going the way of the dodo [an extinct bird]. Only a quarter of women collect pension benefits from their ex-husbands, according to WISER. "Being a woman is a retirement risk," sums up Alicia Munnell, the director of Boston College's Center for Retirement Research.

To be safer, both men and women should save and invest as though they'll live to, say, 95 rather than the 85 that many financial planners recommended as recently as a decade or two ago. And consider your family history. If your grandmother lived to 100, consider buying an annuity, an investment product whose main attraction is payments that last as long as you do.

Periodical Bibliography

The following articles have been selected to supplement the diverse views presented in this chapter.

W. Andrew Achenbaum	"What Is Retirement For?" *Wilson Quarterly*, Spring 2006.
Nicholas Eberstadt and Hans Groth	"Healthy Old Europe," *Foreign Affairs*, May/ June 2007.
The Economist	"How to Deal with a Falling Population," July 28, 2007.
Haya El Nasser	"States Want to Tap Boomers' Skills," *USA Today*, February 22, 2008.
Dinah Eng	"It's Time to Value Older Workers for Experience," *Television Week*, September 17, 2007.
Tim Fischer	"The Crisis in Finding Workers," *Graphic Arts Monthly*, November 2007.
Mary Beth Franklin and Robert Frick	"Retire to Your Dream Job," *Kiplinger's Personal Finance*, April 2008.
Daniel Kadlec	"Enjoy the Climb," *Time*, April 28, 2003.
Beverly Kaye and Joyce Cohen	"Safeguarding the Intellectual Capital of Baby Boomers," *T&D*, April 2008.
William J. Lynott	"How Inflation Will Affect Your Retirement," *Ophthalmology Times*, December 1, 2007.
Grant Schellenberg, Martin Turcotte, and Bali Ram	"Preparing for Retirement," *Canadian Social Trends*, Fall 2005.
Eric Schurenberg	"Why We Flunked 401(k)," *Money*, April 2008.
Roger Scruton	"Where Are the Kids?" *The American Spectator*, November 2007.

CHAPTER 4

What Is the Role of Science in the Aging Process?

Chapter Preface

While issues related to a rapidly growing aged population are fairly recent, the problems of aging itself have been around for a long time. So has the desire to escape aging altogether. Stories of mortals striving for immortality date back over four thousand years, as depicted in ancient Mesopotamia's *Epic of Gilgamesh.*

Only in the past several decades, however, has "solving the problem of aging" moved from the realm of magic and mythology to the world of serious scientific research. One of the first organizations concerned with the issues facing the elderly was the Gerontological Society of America, formed in 1945 to promote the scientific study of aging.

Research on possible life extension through calorie restriction—usually manifested through a diet high in plant foods and containing 30 to 50 percent fewer calories than the typical American eats—began in the 1930s, and was one topic of the 2008 Barbara Walters television special *Live to 150, Can You Do It? Secrets to Living Longer*. To date, the record for the longest human life is just under 122.5 years, but some scientists now believe that 150 years is attainable and potentially even routine.

Other researchers and advocates, however, are aiming much higher. The idea of stopping the physical effects of aging completely, even reversing them, is gaining increasing ground in mainstream science. It has long been known that many cold-blooded species do not age in the sense of reaching a peak physical condition and then automatically beginning to deteriorate. Now researchers hope to find a way to transfer the process to such age-vulnerable species as humans. In 1993, Cynthia Kenyon, a molecular geneticist from the University of California at San Francisco, achieved the first major breakthrough in this area by manipulating the genes of microscopic nematode worms, multiplying their average life spans by two and eventually by six. British gerontologist Aubrey de Grey, one of the most prominent spokesmen for the movement to prolong youth, believes that similar advances applicable to humans are imminent and that science will also likely find ways to reverse aging. He says, "I think the first person to live to 1,000 might be 60 already."

Although even one thousand years is a short span of time compared to the estimated 4.5 billion years that the Earth has existed (or the nearly 14 billion years of the larger universe), the idea of putting a stop to human aging raises several questions, including: Is it really possible, and, is it really a benefit to mankind? The following chapter explores these issues.

> "I expect many people alive today to live to one thousand years of age and to avoid age-related health problems even at that age."

Science Will Soon Be Able to Slow or Stop the Aging Process

Aubrey de Grey and Michael Rae

In the following viewpoint, extreme-longevity advocate and researcher Aubrey de Grey describes his concept of longevity escape velocity (LEV), by which steady progress in increasing human life span would buy time for further advances, and would ultimately stretch life expectancy to hundreds of years. De Grey, chairman and chief science officer of the Methuselah Foundation, believes that science is on the verge of breakthroughs that could make this goal possible within a generation, and that indefinite life extension will ultimately improve quality of life throughout the world. Science and health writer Michael Rae is de Grey's research assistant.

Aubrey de Grey and Michael Rae, "Bootstrapping Our Way to an Ageless Future," *Ending Aging: The Rejuvenation Breakthroughs that Could Reverse Human Aging in Our Lifetime*, New York: St. Martin's Press, 2007, pp. 325–327, 330–334. Copyright © 2007 by Aubrey de Grey. All rights reserved. Reprinted by permission of St. Martin's Press, LLC and the author.

As you read, consider the following questions:

1. According to de Grey, what is the primary difference between maintaining a machine and maintaining a living body?

2. What analogy does de Grey use to illustrate the principle of longevity escape velocity?

3. How does de Grey expect the LEV concept to encourage development of SENS (Strategies for Engineered Negligible Senescence)?

The [anti-aging] therapies that we develop in a decade or so in mice, and those may come only a decade or two later for humans, will not be perfect. Other things being equal, there will be a residual accumulation of damage within our bodies, however frequently and thoroughly we apply these therapies, and we will eventually experience age-related decline and death just as now, only at a greater age. Probably not all that much greater either—probably only thirty to fifty years older than today.

But other things won't be equal. . . . I'm going to explain why not—and why, as you may already know from other sources, I expect many people alive today to live to one thousand years of age and to avoid age-related health problems even at that age.

I'll start by describing why it's unrealistic to expect these therapies to be perfect.

Evolution Did Not Leave Notes

The body is a machine, and that's both why it ages and why in principle it can be maintained. I made a comparison with vintage cars, which are kept fully functional even one hundred years after they were built, using the same maintenance technologies that kept them going fifty years ago when they were already far older than they were ever designed to be. More complex machines can also be kept going indefinitely, though the expense and expertise involved may mean that this never happens in practice because replacing the machine is a reasonable alternative. This sounds very much like a reason to suppose that the therapies we develop to stave off aging for a few decades will indeed be enough to stave it off indefinitely.

The Dangers of Invasive Maintenance

But actually that's overoptimistic. All we can reliably infer from a comparison with man-made machines is that a truly comprehensive panel of therapies, which truly repairs everything that goes wrong with us as a result of aging, is possible *in principle*—not that it is foreseeable. And in fact, one thing about them is very unlike maintenance of a man-made machine: these therapies strive to minimally alter metabolism itself, and target only the initially inert side effects of metabolism, whereas machine maintenance may involve adding extra things to the machinery itself (to the fuel or to the oil of a car, for example). We can get away with this sort of invasive maintenance of man-made machines because we (well, some of us!) know how they work right down to the last detail, so we can be adequately sure that our intervention won't have unforeseen side effects. With the body—even the body of a mouse—we are still profoundly ignorant of the details, so we have to sidestep our ignorance by interfering as little as possible.

Long-Term Aspects of Aging Will Eventually Appear

What that means for efficacy of therapies is that, as we fix more and more aspects of aging, you can bet that new aspects will be unmasked. These new things—eighth and subsequent items to add to the "seven deadly things" [mitochondrial mutations, waste material from cell functions, waste proteins accumulating on tissues, ongoing chemical processes that impede healthy protein functions, potentially cancerous cells, loss of old cells, and DNA mutations]—will not be fatal at a currently normal age, because if they were, we'd know about them already. But they'll be fatal eventually, unless we work out how to fix them, too.

It's not just "eighth things" we have to worry about, either. Within each of the seven *existing* categories, there are some subcategories that will be easier to fix than others. For example, there are lots of chemically distinct cross-links responsible for stiffening our arteries; some of them may be broken with alagebrium [an antiaging drug that is designed to reverse stiffening of blood vessel walls] and related molecules, but others will surely need more sophisticated agents that have not yet been developed. Another example: obviating mitochondrial DNA [mtDNA] by putting modified copies of it into the cell's chromosomes requires gene therapy, and thus far we have no gene therapy delivery system ("vector") that can safely get into all cells, so for the foreseeable future we'll probably only be able to protect a subset of cells from mtDNA mutations. Much better vectors will be needed if we are to reach all cells.

The Dilemma of Diminishing Effectiveness

In practice, therefore, therapies that rejuvenate sixty-year-olds by twenty years will not work so well the second time around. When the therapies are applied for the first time, the people receiving them will have sixty years of "easy" damage (the types that the therapies can remove) and also sixty years of "difficult" damage. But by the time beneficiaries of these therapies have returned to biologically sixty (which, let's presume, will happen when they're chronologically about eighty), the damage their bodies contain will consist of twenty years of "easy" damage and eighty years of "difficult" damage. Thus, the therapies will only rejuvenate them by a much smaller amount, say ten years. So they'll have to come back sooner for the third treatment, but that will benefit them even less . . . and very soon . . . aging will get the better of them. . . .

[But] if we can make rejuvenation therapies work well enough to give us time to make them work better, that will give us enough additional time to make them work better still, which will . . . you get the idea. This will allow us to escape age-related decline indefinitely, however old we become in purely chronological terms. I think the term "longevity escape velocity" (LEV) sums that up pretty well.

Accumulating Lead Time

One feature of LEV that's worth pointing out is that we can accumulate lead time. What I mean is that if we have a period in which we improve the therapies faster than we need to, that will allow us to have a subsequent period in which we don't improve them so fast. It's only the *average* rate of improvement, starting from the arrival of the first therapies that give us just twenty or thirty extra years, that needs to stay above the LEV threshold.

In case you're having trouble assimilating all this, let me describe it in terms of the physical state of the body. I've been discussing aging as the accumulation of molecular and cellular "damage" of various types, and I've highlighted the fact that a modest quantity of damage is no problem metabolism just works around it, in the same way that a household only needs to put out the garbage once a week, not every hour. In those terms, the attainment and maintenance of longevity escape velocity simply means that our best therapies must improve fast enough to outpace the progressive shift in the composition of our aging damage to more repair-resistant forms, as the forms that are easier to repair are progressively eliminated by our therapies. If we can do this, the total amount of damage in each category can be kept permanently below the level that initiates functional decline.

Immortal Cells

Simple single-cell animals, such as the pond-water organism called *Tetrahymena*, abound in our contemporary environment. They, too, like the original assemblies of molecules, are immortal. Unlike you and me, they leave no dead ancestors behind. By this I do not mean that they *cannot* die, only that they are not *programmed* to do so. Hit an immortal cell with a hammer and, yes, it will die. Starve it for food and it will die. "Immortal" in the above sense really means that the cell is *potentially* immortal—that is, that there is nothing inlaid in its DNA that calls for aging—and that, barring accident, and provided it is surrounded with ample nutrition, it can go on living and reproducing forever.

The discovery of the cell had to await the invention of the microscope in the seventeenth century. When scientists turned this instrument on life itself, they saw a world of microscopic entities, cells that carried disease, cells like sperm that were the medium of sexual reproduction. This changed everything. A light shone down and the science of cell biology was born. The new dogma was summarized in Latin as *omnis cellula e cellula*—that is, "all cells arise from preexisting cells," a finding based on an earlier recognition of the continuity of life, that "all life arises from preexisting life."

Michael D. West, The Immortal Cell: One Scientist's Quest to Solve the Mystery of Human Aging, *New York: Doubleday, 2003.*

The Principle of Escape Velocity

Another, perhaps simpler, way of looking at this is to consider the analogy with literal escape velocity, i.e. the overcoming of gravity. Suppose you're at the top of a cliff and you jump off.

Your remaining life expectancy is short—and it gets shorter as you descend to the rocks below. This is exactly the same as with aging: The older you get, the less remaining time you can expect to live. The situation with the periodic arrival of ever better rejuvenation therapies is then a bit like jumping off a cliff with a jet pack on your back. Initially the jet pack is turned off, but as you fall, you turn it on and it gives you a boost, slowing your fall. As you fall farther, you turn up the power on the jet pack, and eventually you start to pull out of the dive and even start shooting upward. And the farther up you go, the easier it is to go even further. . . .

The Problem of Spending Priorities

LEV makes all the difference.

SENS [Strategies for Engineered Negligible Senescence, the major principles of de Grey's antiaging theory] therapies will be expensive to develop and expensive to administer, at least at first. Let's consider how the prospect of spending all that money might be received if the ultimate benefit would be only to add a couple of decades to the lives of people who are already living longer than most in the developing world, after which those people would suffer the same duration of functional decline that they do now.

It's not exactly the world's most morally imperative action, is it?

Indeed, I would go so far as to say that, if I were in control of a few billion dollars, I would be quite hesitant to spend it on such a marginal improvement in the overall quality and quantity of life of those who are already doing better in that respect than most, when the alternative exists of making a similar or greater improvement to the quality and quantity of life of the world's less fortunate inhabitants.

Hope of Soon Achieving LEV

The LEV concept doesn't make much difference in the short term to who would benefit from these therapies, of course: it will necessarily be those who currently die of aging, so in the first instance it will predominantly be those in wealthy nations. But there is a very widespread appreciation in the industrialised world—an appreciation that, I feel, extends to the wealthy sectors of society—that progress in the long term relies on aiming high, and in particular that the moral imperative to help those at the rear of the field to catch up is balanced by the moral imperative to maximize the average rate of progress across the whole population, which initially means helping those who are already ahead. The fact that SENS is likely to lead to LEV means that developing SENS gives a huge boost to the quality and quantity of life of whomever receives it: so huge, in fact, that there is no problem justifying it in comparison to the alternative uses to which a similar sum of money might be put. The fact that life span is extended indefinitely rather than by only a couple of decades is only part of the difference that LEV makes, of course: arguably an even more important difference in terms of the benefit that SENS gives is that the *whole* of that life will be youthful, right up until a beneficiary mistimes the speed of an oncoming truck. The average quality of life, therefore, will rise much more than if all that was in prospect were a shift from, say, 7:1 to 9:1 in the ratio of healthy life to frail life.

> "There comes a time in every life when that knowledge [of our mortality] hits home emotionally. How we react to that realization says a lot about our character."

Science Cannot Stop the Aging Process

Harriet Hall

In the following viewpoint, Harriet Hall reviews three books on medical theories of longevity: Fantastic Voyage *by Ray Kurzweil and Terry Grossman;* Anti-Aging Medicine, *edited by S. Jay Olshansky, Leonard Hayflick, and Thomas T. Perls; and* Healthy Aging *by Andrew Weil. She concludes that* Anti-Aging Medicine, *which emphasizes that there is no magic pill to prolong youth, is the only book of the three that is realistic. Hall denounces* Fantastic Voyage *for its naïve endorsement of dubious antiaging techniques, and criticizes* Healthy Aging *for its uncertain recommendations and metaphysical leanings. Harriet Hall is a physician and resident medical expert for* Skeptic *magazine.*

As you read, consider the following questions:

1. According to Hall, how many nutritional pills does Ray Kurzweil, coauthor of *Fantastic Voyage*, take daily?

Harriet Hall, "Three Perspectives on Longevity: Fantasy, Reality, and Confusion," *Skeptic*, vol. 12, no. 4, 2006, pp. 56–58. Reproduced by permission.

2. What slow-aging techniques does Hall report as being among those critiqued in *Anti-Aging Medicine?*

3. What elements of *Healthy Aging* receive a favorable report from Hall?

Ray Kurzweil is an inventor, thinker and futurist who believes he can live forever, and that you can too if you read his book, *Fantastic Voyage: Live Long Enough to Live Forever.* Since Kurzweil is no crackpot, and he says he has extraordinary science to back up his extraordinary claim, this is fair game for skeptical analysis, starting with the dedication to two of the author's ancestors, one of whom lived to age 104 with no health advice at all (which is an argument against the book) and the other who died at age 58 but "could have been alive today" if he had read this book (a claim for which there is no evidence presented).

Hopes for Immortality Through Technology

At the age of 35 Kurzweil developed diabetes, which jolted him into doing something about his health prospects. He convinced himself that future technology promises immortality and that present knowledge will allow him to survive long enough to take advantage of it. Some day we will understand the genome, have specific prevention for all the processes of aging, and send tiny robots through our veins to fix whatever goes wrong. Eventually we can also stop breathing, replace our blood cells with trillions of more efficient nanobots, and dispense with most of our organs. He describes some fascinating speculations derived from cutting edge research—they're fun to think about and some of them may even come true.

Kurzweil's Personal Program

After extensive research, Kurzweil designed a personal program that he believes will slow his aging processes. He gets virtual colonoscopies, CAT scans, thallium stress tests, "extensive cancer screens" and PSA [prostate-specific antigen] levels. Every few months he gets tested for dozens of nutrient levels (vitamins, minerals, fats, hormones, metabolic by-products). Based on test results, he fine tunes his supplement program. He takes just about every product in the diet supplement market in an effort to "reprogram his bio-chemistry," downing as many as 250 pills of nutritionals a day. Yes, 250 pills a day! For example: acetyl-l-carnitine, vinpocetine, phosphatidylserine, ginkgo biloba, glycerlyphosphorylcholine, nextrutine, and quercetin for brain health and lutein and bilbery extract for eye health. To boost antioxidant levels he takes vitamins, minerals, plus 16 different supplements. In addition to the 250 pills, he also ingests Chinese herbs prescribed by Dr. Glenn Rothfeld. Once a week, he spends the day at a complementary medicine health clinic getting half a dozen IV nutritionals, IV chelation [heavy-metal purges], and acupuncture. He practices weight control, strict (organic) diet, exercise, massage, meditation, seeks balance in life, and keeps his brain active. He avoids toxins, drinks 10 glasses of alkalinized (pH 9.5) water a day, uses an ionic air filter, and has had his mercury amalgam filings removed. He lives in fear of cell phones, shower water, electric razors, plastic, the aluminum in deodorants, and the White Satan: sugar.

Never Met an Idea He Did Not Like

Kurzweil says he avoids "ideas that are unproven or appear to be risky," but I cannot see that he ever met an idea he didn't like. In the entire book, I could only find two things he rejected: [the tranquilizer] kava, and IV human growth hormone (although he does recommend [the steriod prohormone] DHEA). He is walking advertisement for the diet supplement industry.

Kurzweil's co-author is Terry Grossman, an MD who runs a longevity clinic. Grossman became a convert to alternative medicine when pine bark capsule cured his knee pain. "Being a scientist," he verified that the pain went away when he took the pills and returned when he stopped. Of course, he always knew when he was taking them, so we cannot discount placebo. Grossman "only" takes 64 supplement pills a day, plus 24 traditional Chinese medicine pillules prescribed by his wife.

The Limitations of Genomic Testing

Kurzweil and Grossman advocate genomic testing to see what diseases you are susceptible to and to guide your preventive program, but they don't make a good case for it. Genomic testing is in its infancy and many diseases are multifactorial. The factors are complex; they interact with each other and with the environment. The examples they give of personalized advice derived from an individual's genome are not substantially different from the general advice applicable to everyone.

Fantastic Voyage is more like "fantasy" voyage. Kurzweil and Grossman accept the myths that aspartame is harmful and that thorough chewing of food is vital to health, and they believe it is not feasible to get optimal levels of nutrients from food alone. They recommend eliminating wheat from the diet and taking high doses of beta-carotene, which *The Medical Letter* says no one should take. The alkaline water they recommend is called "snake oil on tap" by others and even [integrative medicine advocate] Andrew Weil's website calls it bogus.

A Guinea Pig in an Uncontrolled Experiment

I guess if you try enough things, one of them just might work. On the other hand, there is also a very good chance that the combination of everything but the kitchen sink will do more harm than good. How much do 250 pills weigh? How might the supplements interact? What fillers and other ingredients are in the pills? To follow their advice might be like being a guinea pig in an uncontrolled experience. They're a lot braver than I am.

Kurzweil and Grossman are also convinced that heart disease and the majority of cancers can be prevented by environmental and lifestyle choices. Maybe; but that hasn't been proven. The big mistake they make is to assume that animal and test tube experiments are relevant to humans, and that small preliminary studies can be used to direct therapeutic advice. There's many a slip twixt test tube and clinical practice. Antioxidants have shown all kinds of benefits in the lab, but when you give them to large groups of real people as supplements, they always seem to do more harm than good. And a supplement may change the level of something on a blood test but not have any practical influence on health. Kurzweil and Gross have not discovered the importance of POEMS—Patient Oriented Evidence That Matters. And They obviously haven't read the Quackwatch website [quackwatch.org]! Much of what they recommend has been evaluated and debunked there.

Hope Triumphs Over Evidence

Kurzweil and Grossman also offer pseudoscientific statements with no critical comment: "Shiatsu and acupressure massage are ... intended to correct imbalances according to principles of energy flow between different organ systems in the body." "The elaborate structures formed by water molecules as a result of its electrical field create a form of memory that has been demonstrated by magnetic resonance imaging (MRI) machines."

These guys are obsessed. The book represents the triumph of hope over evidence and common sense. Taking 250 pills a day and worrying about absorbing chlorine through the skin from your shower water are not likely to make you live any longer, although I can see how they might make it seem a lot longer.

Debunking Anti-Aging Claims

Now for a more sober view of rigorously scientific thinking about anti-aging medicine: Jay Olshansky, Leonard Hayflick, and Thomas T. Perls say there's no such thing. Their edited volume, *Anti-Aging Medicine: The Hype and the Reality*, is a compendium of papers by respected scientists who study the aging process and treat the elderly. They conclude: "There is no intervention known to slow, stop, or reverse the fundamental aging process in humans." Anti-aging quackery is rampant in today's marketplace, and the use of human growth hormone (HGH) to slow aging is actually illegal There is concern about the safety of supplements and of medications like natural hormones. The use of micronutrient and antioxidants supplements is not supported by the literature. "Systems that suggest the ability of bio-markers of aging and agents to favorably affect them are not scientifically based."

That pretty well shoots *Fantastic Voyage* all to hell!

The Complexities of Aging

The authors—all experts on the biology of aging—go on to discuss the complexities of the processes we lump together as "aging," the philosophical and sociological consequences that would result from life extension, the status of current research, and other fascinating subjects, presenting debates with both pro and con arguments and rebuttals.

Healthy Aging

What does America's leading integrative medicine guru Andrew Weil have to say on the subject of aging and longevity? In *Healthy Aging* he agrees that "There are no anti-aging medicines. Scientific evidence is incomplete at best, and totally lacking at worst, for all of the products and services." He gives an example of the kind of faulty thinking Kurzweil uses: [the nutritional supplement] resveratrol makes yeast cells live longer. It's "possible" that it might do the same for people.

Immortality Is Unlikely

The "victory over mortality" is a canard. No serious scientist believes victory over mortality is possible. We may someday be able to slow down the aging process, but reversing it is unlikely, and engineering the germ line to attain greater life span represents a risky form of human experimentation few if any societies on earth would be willing to undertake. . . .

In a recent publication, the International Longevity Center suggested that "large increases in life expectancy to 150 years or more in humans, as often suggested by antiaging entrepreneurs, may be unrealistic without major new insights into the molecular mechanisms of aging." Needless to say, those "major new insights" have yet to appear. Leonard Hayflick and a number of other prominent gerontologists have become so annoyed by the claims of life-extension enthusiasts that they recently prepared a manifesto. . . .

"The prospect of immortality," the scientists state, "is no more likely today than it has ever been, and it has no place in a scientific discourse."

Stephen S. Hall, Merchants of Immortality: Chasing the Dream of Human Life Extension, *Boston: Houghton Mifflin, 2003.*

"Without much more evidence to support their case, resveratrol enthusiasts have leapt to just this conclusion." Weil does not mince words:

These are the hard facts. It is theoretically possible to extend the human life span, but no methods of doing so are currently available. We do not really even know if calorie restriction will do it for us. Furthermore, it is unlikely that any such methods will become available in time for anyone reading this book to make use of them.

. . . these theoretical breakthroughs serve only as serious distractions from what's important, namely, learning to accept the universality and inevitability of aging, understanding both its challenges and promises, and knowing how to keep minds and bodies as healthy as possible as we move through life's successive stages.

Off to a Good Start

Weil teaches us how to age gracefully and maintain balance in our lives. He gives good advice about prevention: weight, smoking, immunizations, appropriate screening tests, the limitations of some screening tests like prostate-specific antigen (PSA) and computed tomography (CT) calcium screening for heart disease.

So far, so good. If he had had the sense to stop there, *Healthy Aging* would have been an excellent book.

Unfortunately, Weil goes on to mix sense with silliness, medicine with metaphysics, as he does indiscriminately in his previous books.

Weil thinks we should eat more plants, even "natural toxins" such as betel, qat, opium, coca, coffee, tea, chocolate, kava, and marijuana, because these may help bolster our defenses against oxidative stress. Should we supplement with antioxidants? "Not only is there insufficient evidence that taking them will do you any good, some experts think they might be harmful." But he throws reason to the winds and takes them anyway. Multivitamins, Co-Q-10, grape seed extract and pine bark extract, alpha-lipoic acid, ginger, turmeric, DHEA, a medley of immune-enhancing mushrooms (Weil has always had a fondness for mushrooms, psychedelic and otherwise) astragalus, milk thistle, ginseng, arctic root, and Cordyceps. He says all these definitely work and are safe. The scientific consensus begs to differ.

The Medical Mystic

Weil says evidence based medicine "discounts the evidence of experience." As he explains: "I maintain that it is possible to look at the world scientifically and also to be aware of non-material reality." He speaks of qi and prana unquestioningly, saying breath is the link to this basic life energy that circulates through us. He recommends specific breathing exercises, body work, massage and meditation. He trusts intuition; he believes in multiple realities.

Weil concludes: "I believe in magic and mystery. I am also committed to scientific method and knowledge based on evidence. How can this be? I have told you that I operate from a *both-and* mentality, not an *either-or* one." He thinks consciousness is primary, more basic than matter or energy, and he thinks it directs the evolution of the material universe (huh?). He offers no evidence to support this claim.

Oh, by the way, he sells the supplements he recommends.

The Intellectual and the Emotional

Intellectually, we all know that life ends in death; but there comes a time in every life when that knowledge hits home emotionally. How we react to that realization says a lot about our character. These three books represent three very different approaches.

Kurzweil is a denier who is running scared and wants to believe he can cheat death. He is brilliant in his own field, but is a poor judge of medical studies. He has fallen into the same trap Linus Pauling did when he aggressively promoted vitamin C and orthomolecular medicine on the basis of preliminary evidence that was later discredited. It is sad to see a good intellect fall prey to obsessions and delusions; it is sadder to see those delusions aided and abetted by a medical doctor in a folie a deux [similar delusions present in two closely associated persons]; it is sadder still when books are published encouraging others to share their delusions.

Weil is much more realistic, but he is incapable of sticking strictly to the evidence and insists on the validity of his intuitive insights. He goes beyond the facts and asks us to trust him because he thinks he is smarter than unaided science.

Firmly Grounded in Reality

Anti-Aging Medicine is the only one that stays firmly grounded in the realm of science and critical thinking. The reality is that we don't yet know how to prolong our lifespan. We can spend our allotted time popping pills and worrying about the aluminum in our deodorant, or we can relax, follow the most up-to-date solid science (in moderation), and try to get the most possible enjoyment out of the years we have left.

One of my college professors used to say that your age has very little to do with the number of years you have lived. My grandmother said when she realized she had a 65-year old son she knew she must *be* old, but she still didn't *feel* old inside. Most of us would like to live as long as possible, but we can accept death as an integral part of life; knowing that we are going to die makes life just that much more precious. Personally, I plan to eat a variety of non-organic foods, drink unalkalinized tap water, stay active, indulge in a little White Satanic sugar, eschew diet supplements, and find something more interesting to do than taking 250 pills a day.

> "To best pursue happiness, individually and as a group, we need unbounded vitality and excitement, not a grim wait for a meaningless and thoroughly preventable end."

Indefinitely Prolonging Life Would Be Desirable

Michael Anissimov

By late 2002, Leon Kass, University of Chicago biomedical ethicist and chair of the George W. Bush administration's Council on Bioethics, had become well known for his stance against scientific attempts to induce immortality and for his insistence that indefinite life spans would be conducive to overpopulation, social inequity, ennui, and the destruction of high moral principles. The following viewpoint by Michael Anissimov, former advocacy director for the Singularity Institute for Artificial Intelligence and North American fundraising director for the scientific and humanitarian Lifeboat Foundation, offers one rebuttal to several of Kass's opinions.

Michael Anissimov, "Objections to Immortality: Answering Leon Kass," *Working Towards Apotheosis*, February 2003. www.acceleratingfuture.com/michael/works/answeringkass.htm. Reproduced by permission.

As you read, consider the following questions:

1. What technologies does Anissimov cite as holding potential for human life extension?
2. How does Anissimov answer Kass's assertion that life extension would widen the gap between rich and poor?
3. According to Anissimov, what is the "one reason" for the current limited human life span?

How far can we push life extension? A panoply of technologies currently under development could, in principle, extend the human lifespan indefinitely. Deaths in accidents may continue to be possible, but there's no physical law that would necessarily prevent a human's body from being immortal by design. A triple wave of future advances—sophisticated biotechnology, medical nanotechnology, and artificial intelligence—all offer powerful theoretical and practical arguments for the achievability of immortality.

The Sciences of Endless Life

Biotechnology, such as in gene therapy, telomere-extension [chromosome-protecting DNA], or the cheap manufacture of replacement organs, is a continuously growing area of research, but is also one of the most ethically troublesome areas of research, and therefore is heavily regulated by conservative policymakers. The Life Extension Foundation is a good example of an organization focusing primarily on the biological approach to immortality. Medical nanotechnology entails the control of large groups of molecular-scale machines, which could enter the body noninvasively and regularly repair biological damage on a fine-grained level, before it can accrete. The Foresight Institute, most notably the researcher Robert Freitas Jr., is widely known for studying the technical and political aspects of medical nanotechnology, among other types of nanotechnology. Creating benevolent self-improving artificial intelligence [AI] is the pursuit of the Singularity Institute for Artificial Intelligence, a research project aiming to create genuine transhumanity by exploiting the unique cognitive advantages a general AI would have relative to humans. These cognitive resources could rapidly be applied in humanitarian areas, such as life extension research, with rapidly effective results (from the human perspective). The Immortality Institute and the Extropy Institute are additional organizations representing proponents of scientific immortality from a variety of different approaches and perspectives.

But the pursuit of radical life extension, of course, is not without opponents, and there exist a number of prominent individuals in politics and science who see longer lifespans as undesirable and threatening to the spirit of man. Perhaps the most active of these individuals is Leon Kass, the head of [George W.] Bush's Presidential Bioethics Council, who has given numerous talks about the perils and foreignness of human life extension and lobbies for intense regulation in this area. . . .

Firstly, Kass argues that if everyone overcame aging it could lead to negative social consequences, a "Tragedy of the Commons" that could include such things as overpopulation and skewed demographics.

Challenges Are Not to Be Avoided

Widespread extreme life extension will most definitely reshape the fabric of society in profound ways, but these are challenges that will need to be faced head on, not avoided. A society with the technological capacity to overcome aging is also extremely likely to possess other useful technologies that will soften or eliminate the negative social impact of widespread life extension usage. Profound social and technological events (such as the rise of capitalism or the invention of cheap aircraft) have had unique impacts in the past, challenging societies to reform and adapt to these inevitable milestones along the path of man's moral and technological development.

Scientific Immortality as a "Leap of Faith"

When asked if he was worried that one day the [cryonic] company [Alcop] would go out of business and his body might be thawed out and abandoned, or that the technology for reanimation may never be perfected, he [Internet entrepreneur Steven Vachani] said no. [In 2002, Vachani signed up for the Alcorplan, whereby his body will be frozen in liquid nitrogen for £120,000.]

"In doing anything like this, there's a certain leap of faith you have to take," Vachani said. "They don't have all the answers right now, but everything will fall into place. If you want all the answers immediately, you'll never do anything."

Kristen Philipkoski,
"Who Wants to Live Forever?"
Wired, *November 20, 2002.*

Many of the issues presented by life extension are issues already in need of an urgent solution, such as the overpopulation problem or diminishing fossil fuels, and where advances are already starting to be made. Extreme life extension isn't liable to introduce any new fundamental problems that we wouldn't have had to deal with to begin with, and will in fact correct the problems of aging and death, which limit human choice in our own lives. A growing technological civilization must ultimately address these issues whether or not extreme life extension becomes available in the near future. Near-term progress in genetic engineering, nanotechnology, cognitive science, and artificial intelligence will increase mankind's problem-solving capacity and enable us to better confront current or forthcoming problems along the imminent route of technological acceleration ahead of us.

Nanotechnology as a Means of Coping with Overpopulation

For example, the researcher Eric K. Drexler has already developed extensive theoretical arguments for the feasibility of nanotechnology, a bottom-up manufacturing technology which will allow the synthesis of cheap food and housing from raw materials for extremely low costs. This technology could also be applied towards the construction of cheap spacecraft or space elevators, giving millions or billions of individuals the opportunity to colonize the solar system should the Earth become uncomfortably overpopulated. Marshall T. Savage has estimated in his book *The Millennial Project* that the Solar System could sustain upwards of a billion humans, each with mansions upon mansions of living space, for several billion years. This book also neglects the more recently-conceived benefits that advanced nanotechnology and virtual reality would confer once they mature.

For better or for worse, widespread demand for extreme life extension will surface once people are convinced of its possibility, and there would be no greater social injustice than to withhold that privilege from them. Unless vast sectors of scientific and technological research are completely shut down or dictatorially regulated, progress will continue and we will have to confront these changes. Longer and longer lifespans will incrementally emerge due to better nutrition, medicine, and a more widespread, sophisticated, scientific awareness of what factors add or subtract from living a long, healthy, happy life. To place some arbitrary cap on lifespan due to an anticipation of future society's ineptness at handling the challenge is not only morbidly pessimistic, but robs everyday people of their right to live and pursue happiness indefinitely.

Will Life Extension Aggravate Social Inequities?

Secondly, Kass worries that life extension technologies will widen the gap between the rich and the poor, leading to greater social inequities and an overall regression in society's well-being.

Even if life extension would initially be more accessible to the wealthy, the advantage that the rich would derive from such access would be transient and fleeting—historically, novel technological innovations quickly filter down to the masses, and excepting the case of coordinated global action, extreme life extension will be no exception. This becomes especially true in the case of life extension implemented by nanotechnology or artificial intelligence, where the tools one would use to repair the deterioration of their own body are indistinguishable from the tools they would use to simply cure a disease, mend a broken limb, or conduct a variety of other medical tasks. A postulated scenario in which the rich are able to obtain longer lives and the masses are not for a sufficiently long duration as to contribute appreciably to social inequality assumes that extreme life extension is obtained and all other progress miraculously screeches to a halt, or life extension is globally outlawed and rich people only use it in secret, or other such equally unlikely scenarios. By observing technological patterns in society today, we can see that the cost of various medical procedures and life-enhancing tools is falling at faster and faster rates; in fact, the emotional and personal importance of such technologies place an even stronger pressure on companies to make them available as opposed to technologies which are merely conveniences.

Economic Differences Could Prove a Non-Issue

The dynamic flow of progress and capitalism will continue to make technologies available to individuals who are willing to work for them, and create the attendant legal and social frameworks necessary to accommodate these changes. In the instance of immortality implemented through self-replicating nanotechnology, economic divide could actually prove a non-issue due to an influx of abundance; and while I certainly respect due skepticism with regard to more radical technologies such as nanotechnology, the economic divide that many are proposing wouldn't just require huge classes of projected technologies being somehow stifled or regulated out of existence, but the reverse of millennia of accrued advances in politics, economics, and other social structures.

Thirdly, Kass argues that we'd lose interest and engagement in life if it went on forever, a sort of "immortalists' enuui" that postulates that life is only worth living if it is short.

This sentiment seems to entail a very morbid view on life. If a member of an elderly couple is on the verge of death when a new life extension technology becomes available, and this couple decides they want to continue to be together, is it right to deny the continuance of their love on such arbitrary grounds? We didn't lose interest and engagement in life when average lifespan increased from 30 to 70, in fact, thanks to the explosion of culture and technology; there are more exciting things to do than ever before. Cheaper and more effective medical technologies are extending health span as well as lifespan, ensuring that becoming older doesn't mean becoming more senile.

The Original Cause of Limited Lifespan

Our current lifespan has its characteristic length due to one reason, and one reason only; it was the optimal engineering solution on nature's evolutionary payoff curve for maximizing the adaptiveness of our species—for evolution to build humans capable of living longer, there needs to be an immediate fitness advantage, i.e., a reproductive benefit. These selection pressures did not present themselves during our evolution, hence the average ancestral lifespan of about 25 years. "Investing more resources" in human longevity would be useless unless long-living humans could outcompete their rivals in the ancestral environment, and diverting the preexisting resources from longevity would have resulted in humans whose lifespans were too short to outcompete others. But now these evolutionary/adaptive reasons are obsolete—humans don't live in environments like we did when we evolved, and we have no reason to accept nature's limit on our lifespan or healthspan unless we decide that for ourselves. Our particular lifespan is just the consequence of a·set of overlapping constraints which produced the human body, constraints without any cosmic purpose. Humans have already resisted and overcome our default biological limitations through medicine, science, social engineering, government, the postal system, the Internet, and so on. The technologies which will soon enable us to indefinitely lengthen our lives are just natural extensions of the preexisting human drive for progress and happiness. And with the opportunity to enhance our minds as well as our bodies, we will create societies so complex and interesting that our attention or engagement will never run dry.

Social systems would, in time, adapt to the changes that life extension will bring. We live our lives for the future of our children and our children's children, why not also live our lives for our future selves, if we had the chance? Longer lives will encourage people living in the present to address the problems of the future, and will also contribute to a heightened sense of moral responsibility, because many will choose to be continuously moral rather than escape our transgressions through death. . . .

The Relationship Between Mortality and Morality

Lastly, Kass argues that mortality is necessary for virtue and morality (we couldn't sacrifice our lives for something if we were immortal).

While it is true that some aspects of our present-day consensus morality do probably rest upon limited lifespan, the injustice of nonconsensual death far overwhelms the small portions of our morality which will be thrown off balance with the introduction of extreme life extension. In a society with longer lifespans and greater overall safety, mortality is playing a smaller and smaller part in the overall picture of morality, and the consensus view on morality has been incrementally changing to reflect this. The consensus view of morality will continue to change to accommodate these humanitarian advances. In almost every case, it's easier to do more good if one is able to live longer, than through sacrifice.

The Advantages of Public Debate

My conclusion is clear; the world needs more life, not less, in order to prosper. To best pursue happiness, individually and as a group, we need unbounded vitality and excitement, not a grim wait for a meaningless and thoroughly preventable end. On the plus side, criticism from people like Kass shows that the prospect of immortality is being taken seriously. A few decades ago, the very notion of indefinite lifespan for humans, no matter what the enabling technology, was considered relatively crazy. So the situation is improving. Now that the mainstream of society is starting to consider the consequences of extended lifespan, immortalists should take the opportunity to speak out and affirm their rights to life, because these rights may be in immediate danger. The time of leverage is now: in the coming decade, many foundational decisions will be made which will lay the groundwork for the future context of the debate. The best way for one to extend their lifespan in today's world is not necessarily through diet, exercise, or supplements, but through advocating the right ideas and actively navigating to the best of all possible futures.

> "I cannot imagine that the consequences of ... [prolonging life much beyond a hundred years] will be anything but baleful, not only for each of us as an individual, but for every other living creature in our world."

Indefinitely Prolonging Life Would Not Be Desirable

Sherwin B. Nuland

While doing research for the MIT Technology Review *in 2004, Sherwin B. Nuland spent two days interviewing longevity researcher Aubrey de Grey, calling him "one remarkable man, whose vision [for the human life span] reaches far beyond a mere few centuries of life ... perhaps [to] eternity." In the following viewpoint, Nuland explains why he disagrees with the philosophy behind de Grey's ideas. Nuland is a clinical professor of surgery at Yale University; he has written numerous books, including* How We Die *and* The Art of Aging, *from which this viewpoint was excerpted.*

As you read, consider the following questions:

1. According to Nuland, what breakthrough does de Grey expect will "kick-start a 'War on Aging?'"

2. Nuland admits that de Grey's vision includes several life choices intriguing even to skeptics. Which of these choices are noted in the viewpoint?

3. Regarding which of de Grey's ideas does Nuland state, "I have more confidence in human nature than to believe that"?

I have no desire to live beyond the life span that nature has granted to our species. For reasons that are pragmatic, scientific, demographic, economic, political, social, emotional, and secularly spiritual, I am committed to the notion that both individual fulfillment and the ecological balance of life on this planet are best served by dying when our inherent biology decrees that we do. I am equally committed to having that age be, as close as modern biomedicine will allow, our biologically probable maximum of approximately 120 years, and I'm also committed to efforts at decreasing and compressing the years of morbidity and disabilities now attendant on extreme old age. But I cannot imagine that the consequences of doing a single thing beyond this will be anything but baleful, not only for each of us as an individual, but for every other living creature in our world. Another action I cannot imagine is enrolling myself—as has de Grey—with Alcor, the cryogenics company that will, for a price, preserve a customer's head or more until that hoped-for day when it can be brought back to some form of life. . . .

De Grey does have some interesting notions of human nature. On the one hand, he insists that it is basic to humankind to want to live forever regardless of consequences, while on the other it is not basic to want to have children. When I protested that the two most formative driving forces of all living things are to survive and to pass on their DNA, he quickly made good use of the one and denied the existence of the other. Bolstering his argument by the observation that many people choose—like Adelaide and himself—not to have children, he replied, not without a hint of petulance and some small bit of excited waving of his hands:

> Your precept is that we all have the fundamental impulse to reproduce. The incidence of voluntary childlessness is exploding. Therefore the imperative to reproduce is not actually so deep-seated as psychologists would have us believe. It may simply be that it was the thing to do—the more traditional thing. My point of view is that a large part of it may simply be indoctrination. . . . I'm not in favor of giving young girls dolls to play with, because it may perpetuate the urge to motherhood.

De Grey has commented in several forums on his conviction that, given the choice, the great majority of people would choose life extension over having children and the usual norms of family life. This being so, far fewer children would be born. He did not hesitate to say the same to me:

> We will realize there is an overpopulation problem, and if we have the sense we'll decide to fix it [by not reproducing] sooner rather than later, because the sooner we fix it the more choice we'll have about how we live and where we live and how much space we will have and all that. Therefore, the question is, what will we do? Will we decide to live a long time and have fewer children, or will we decide to reject these rejuvenation therapies in order that we can have children? It seems pretty damn clear to me that we'll take the former option, but the point is that I don't know and I don't need to know.

Of course, de Grey's reason for not needing to know is that same familiar imperative he keeps returning to, the imperative that everyone is entitled to choice regardless of the possible consequences. What we need to know, he argues, can be found out after the fact, to be dealt with when it appears;

without choice, we deprive humankind of its most basic liberty. It should not be surprising that a man as insistently individualistic—and as uncommon a sort—as he is would emphasize freedom of personal choice far more than he addresses the potentially toxic harvest that might result from cultivating that dangerous seed in isolation. As with every other of his formulations, this one—the concept of untrammeled freedom of choice for the individual—is taken out of the context of its biological and societal surroundings. Like everything else, it is treated in vitro rather than in vivo. All of the de Grey formulations are based on the great assumption that biology and culture work this way. . . .

He has laid out a schedule projecting the timeline on which he would like to see certain milestone events reached.

The first of these milestones is to control the aging of experimental mice sufficiently to triple their life expectancy. He believes adequate funding will make this doable "ten years from now; almost certainly not as soon as seven years, but very likely to be less than twenty years." Such an accomplishment, de Grey believes, will "kick-start a 'War on Aging'" and will be "the trigger for enormous social upheaval." In an article for the *Annals of the New York Academy of Sciences* in 2002 listing seven coauthors after his own name, de Grey wrote, "We contend that the impact on public opinion and (inevitably) public policy of unambiguous aging-reversal in mice would be so great that whatever work remained necessary at that time to achieve adequate somatic gene therapy would be hugely accelerated." Not only that, he asserts, but the public enthusiasm following upon such a feat will cause many people to begin making life choices based on the probability that they too can reach an equivalent number of years. Such life choices include several that even a skeptic like me would look on with pleasure: For example, when people know that they may live as long as four to five hundred years (with ongoing research during that time sure to add multiples of such

"Wanted to Live Forever—Died Trying," cartoon by *Mark Lynch*, CartoonStock.com.

a figure), they will take fewer chances of involving themselves in anything that might kill them, like wars, crime, bad driving habits, and other hazardous activities. Not only that, but when death of a disease such as influenza is considered premature at the age of two hundred, the urgency to solve the problems of infectious disease will massively increase government and drug company funding in that area.

In addition to accelerating demand for the appropriate research on human applications, the survival of a nine-year-old mouse born to live a third that long is projected to bring in new sources of funding. Because governments and drug companies tend to favor research that promises useful results in a relatively short time, de Grey is not counting on them as a source. He is relying on an infusion of private money to supply the approximately one hundred million dollars per year that he estimates it will take to successfully fight his "war." It is his contention that once mouse-success has been achieved, billionaires will come forward, intent on living as long as possible and having the personal means to support the studies that might make it happen.

Of course, such an optimistic visionary would hardly call attention to the likelihood that quite the opposite effect might result from the appearance of a photograph of his long-lived mouse on the front page of every newspaper in the world. Is it conceivable that such an event would be greeted with the unalloyed enthusiasm of a unanimous public universally eager to open an unlabeled can of worms and begin eating its contents with such voracious appetite as he predicts? I doubt it. More likely, one man's acclaim would be at least one other man's horror. Ethicists, economists, sociologists, members of the clergy, and many worried scientists can be counted on to join huge numbers of thoughtful citizens in a reaction the likes of which would make the present uproar over human cloning seem like a genteel tea party. But, of course, if we are to accept the line of reasoning that follows so logically from de Grey's first principle, that the desire to live forever trumps every other factor in human decision-making, then self-interest—or what some, including me, might call narcissism—will win out in the end. I have more confidence in human nature than to believe that.

De Grey projects that fifteen years beyond the mouse may be enough time in which to reach the goal of tripling human life expectancy, though he concedes that it may take as long as a century. What he does not concede, of course, is that it is more likely not to happen at all. He cannot seem to imagine—considering all the realistic pitfalls along the way—that the odds are heavily against him. And he also cannot seem to imagine that not only the odds but society itself may not come out in his favor. So convinced is he that the inborn urge to conquer death is sufficiently strong that it supersedes any other consideration—including the possibility of destroying our civilization, just the thing that is meant to be enhanced— that he will provide any listener or reader with a string of reasons (more like rationalizations) to explain away why it is that most mainstream gerontologists remain so conspicuously absent from the ranks of those cheering him on. Despite his publicized face and the increasingly loud fanfare that attends some of his pronouncements, he has safeguarded himself against the informed criticism that one might reasonably expect should give him cause to rethink some of his proposals. He has accomplished this self-protection by constructing a personal worldview in which he is made inviolate. He stubbornly refuses to budge a millimeter; he will not give ground to the possibility that any of the barriers to his success may prove to be insuperable.

Many decades ago, in my naïveté and ignorance, I used to think that the ultimate destruction of our planet would be by the neutral power of celestial catastrophe: collision with a gigantic meteor, the burning out of the sun—that sort of thing. In time, I came to believe that the end of days would be by the malevolence of a mad dictator who would unleash an arsenal of explosive or biological weaponry: nuclear bombs, engineered microorganisms—that sort of thing. But my notion of the nature of "that sort of thing" has recently been changing. If we are to be destroyed, I have now become convinced, it will not be a neutral or malevolent force that will do us in, but one that is benevolent in the extreme, one whose only motivation is to improve us and better our civilization.

If we are ever immolated or ever self-immolate, it will be by the efforts of well-meaning scientists who are convinced that they have our best interests at heart. We already know who they are. They are the DNA-tweakers who would enhance us by allowing each set of parents to choose the genetic makeup of their descendants unto every succeeding generation ad infinitum, heedless of the possibility that breeding out variety may alter factors necessary for the survival of our species and its relationship to every form of life on earth; they are the biogerontologists who study extreme caloric restriction in mice and promise us an expectancy extended by 20 percent of a peculiarly nourished existence; they are those other biogerontologists who emerge from their laboratories of molecular science every evening optimistic that they have come just a bit closer to their goal of having us live 250 years by engineering genes, adjusting telomerase, or some other such strategy, downplaying the unanticipated havoc at both the cellular and societal levels that might be wrought by their proposed manipulations.

And now, finally, it is the unique and strangely alluring figure of Aubrey de Grey, who, orating, writing, and striding tirelessly through our midst and the midst of some less-than-fully convinced sympathizers, proclaims like the disheveled herald of a new-begotten future that our most inalienable right is to have the choice of living as long as we wish. With the passion of a single-minded zealot crusading against time, he has issued the ultimate challenge, I believe, to our entire concept of the meaning of humanness. And paradoxically, his clarion call to action is the message of neither a madman nor a bad man, but of a brilliant, beneficent man of good will, who wants only for civilization to fulfill the highest hopes he has for its future. It is a good thing that his grand design will almost certainly not succeed. Were it otherwise, he would surely destroy us in attempting to preserve us.

Periodical Bibliography

The following articles have been selected to supplement the diverse views presented in this chapter.

Robert H. Binstock   "The War on 'Anti-Aging Medicine,'" *The Gerontologist*, 2003.

David Ewing Duncan   "The Enthusiast," *Technology Review*, September/October 2007.

The Economist   "How to Live Forever," January 5, 2008.

Rachel Grumman   "The Ultimate Anti-Aging Vitamin," *Health*, March 2008.

Harvard Men's Health Watch   "DHEA and Health: More Questions than Answers," April 2007.

Michele Mishto, Elena Bellavista, Aurelia Santoro, and Claudio Franceschi   "Proteasome Modulation in Brain: A New Target for Anti-Aging Drugs?" *Central Nervous System Agents in Medicinal Chemistry*, December 2007.

Fernando Suárez Müller   "On Futuristic Gerontology: A Philosophical Evaluation of Aubrey de Grey's SENS Project," *International Journal of Applied Philosophy*, Fall 2007.

Laura Petrecca   "Men Arm Themselves with Anti-Aging Weapons," *USA Today*, April 15, 2008.

Jason Pontin   "Is Defeating Aging a Dream?" *Technology Review*, July 2006.

Glenn Harlan Reynolds   "The End of Aging?" *Popular Mechanics*, March 2008.

Catherine Saint Louis   "Applying a Balm to the Years," *New York Times*, May 13, 2008.

Gregory Stock, Daniel Callahan, and Aubrey de Grey   "Debate: The Ethics of Life Extension," *Rejuvenation Research*, September 2007.

For Further Discussion

Chapter 1

1. Margaret Morganroth Gullette claims that the aging population, frequently treated as useless and pushed out of the productive sector in favor of younger workers, is in danger of sinking into general depression and demoralization. David Oliver Relin, by contrast, reports that the vast majority of people over sixty are still enjoying life, and are demanding and frequently receiving greater respect from their juniors. Which position do you find more credible? Why?

2. Andrew Weil says that the common reaction to aging is to deny it: to consider visible manifestations ugly, hide physical evidence through cosmetics or surgery, and insist on continuing a level of physical activity the body may no longer be able to handle. Stacie Stukin, however, says that while older people are definitely taking care of their health and looks, fewer are resorting to radical approaches, and more are concentrating on making the best of whatever ages they are. Which viewpoint do you find more persuasive? Whose credentials offer better qualifications for a well-informed yet objective conclusion: Weil's as an integrative-medicine specialist, or Stukin's as an independent journalist?

3. Brenda L. Plassman and her colleagues, having studied 856 adults over age seventy, found that more than 20 percent have some degree of significant mental decline. However, Laura L. Carstensen, another university-based researcher, emphasizes findings that state that mental function does not significantly decline with age. Whose argument do you find more convincing, and why?

Chapter 2

1. Chuck Hagel insists that Social Security and other government-funded programs for seniors, while they must be adjusted to reflect longer life spans, will remain necessary to ensure the financial well-being of people no longer able to work. Robin J. Klay and Todd P. Steen argue that far more radical reforms are needed, particularly reforms that encourage the current working population to assume responsibility for their own post-retirement financial needs rather than relying on the younger generation to help fund these programs. What do you think is the best approach to reforming Social Security? Why?

2. Conn Hallinan and Carl Bloice emphasize the potential for a medical crisis as a growing senior population faces decreasing numbers of geriatric doctors and relatively few people who understand the needs of the aged. Mark Schlesinger and Jacob S. Hacker focus on the more positive side of the medical system's changing relationship to an aging population, specifically on the potential advantages of "hybridized" Medicare. Do you think that medicine and government understand and try to meet the health needs of seniors? Why or why not?

3. *The Economist* argues that continuing the age-based system of retirement is impractical in a world of increased longevity and vigor. James H. Schulz and Robert H. Binstock counter that the large majority of the population wants to maintain the current retirement age, and that there are other solutions to a shrinking labor pool. Which argument do you find more persuasive? How might *The Economist*'s focus on the global situation, and Schulz and Binstock's on the national one, affect the overall credibility of their opinions?

Chapter 3

1. Kathy Krepcio says that, even though much of the aging population continues working past traditional retirement age, enough employees will leave the workforce at one time to cause major economic strain on society. Conversely, Ken Dychtwald and his coauthors state that imminent massive retirements by the baby boom generation need not cause harm to the economy because many seniors will choose to remain in the workforce. Do you think that people sixty-five and older are more likely to continue working because they want to, or because they need to? What factors may contribute to a person's remaining in the workforce past retirement age? What are the advantages employers have in hiring older workers?

2. Faisal Islam contends that the soon-to-retire segment of the population not only has had it financially easier all their lives than the generation following, but will be comfortably supported in retirement—through the younger generation's tax dollars and Social Security donations putting even more financial strain on younger workers. Suzanne Perry and Michael Aft, by contrast, emphasize the potential benefits to society when a large retired population becomes available for community service. Do you think most retirees would rather "take it easy" or "give back to society?" Use the viewpoints to support your answer.

3. Jeffrey R. Kosnett believes that, in the face of an unstable economy, it is important to invest in retirement accounts, 401(k) retirement plans, and various other forms of savings and investments. Cait Murphy and her coauthors contend that these typical ways of investing may not ensure sufficient retirement income for those who fail to consider changes in the economy, government policies, and individual health needs. In your opinion, what is the best ap-

proach to retirement planning, and do you think it is possible to "save too much?" Why or why not?

Chapter 4

1. Aubrey de Grey believes that a medical solution to aging is not only possible but likely imminent. Harriet Hall, by contrast, states that numerous respected scientists have concluded that antiaging medicine is a myth. Both authors have educational credentials and recognized expertise. In deciding which viewpoint is more credible, consider how each author's ideals and worldview may color his or her opinion. For instance, de Grey has devoted years to the goal of "ending aging" and is chair of a foundation dedicated to that purpose; while Hall is a resident expert for a publication that emphasizes skepticism regarding controversial claims.

2. Michael Anissimov, arguing in favor of indefinitely prolonging life, contends that related social problems would not be insurmountable and that the benefits of physical immortality outweigh the deeper meaning, beauty, and nobility many people find in death. Sherwin B. Nuland disagrees, insisting that "both individual fulfillment and the ecological balance of life on this planet are best served by dying when our inherent biology decrees that we do." Whom do you find more persuasive? If it were possible to forever maintain your current age and physical condition, would you choose to do so? Why or why not?

Organizations to Contact

The editors have compiled the following list of organizations concerned with the issues debated in this book. The descriptions are derived from materials provided by the organizations. All have publications or information available for interested readers. The list was compiled on the date of publication of the present volume; the information provided here may change. Readers need to remember that many organizations take several weeks or longer to respond to inquiries.

AARP
601 E St. NW, Washington, DC   20049
(888) 687-2277
e-mail: member@aarp.org
Web site: www.aarp.org

AARP (American Association of Retired Persons) is a nonprofit organization dedicated to ensuring ongoing quality of life for those fifty and older, and to bringing about positive social change on issues concerning older citizens. It publishes the bimonthly *AARP The Magazine*, which boasts the world's largest circulation; the English/Spanish magazine *AARP Segunda Juventud*; and the *AARP Bulletin Today*.

Gerontological Society of America (GSA)
1220 L St. NW, Suite 901, Washington, DC   20005
(202) 842-1275 • fax: (202) 842-1150
e-mail: geron@geron.org
Web site: www.geron.org

The Gerontological Society of America is a nonprofit organization with over five thousand members who work in aging-related fields. An information provider for researchers, educators, and politicians, GSA's goal is to use basic and applied research on aging to improve the quality of life for seniors. It publishes the monthly *Gerontology News*, accessible in pdf format through the GSA Web site.

Harvard School of Public Health-MetLife Foundation Initiative on Retirement & Civic Engagement
Center for Health Communication
Harvard School of Public Health
677 Huntington Ave., Suite 329, Boston, MA   02115
(617) 432-1038 • fax: (617) 731-8184
e-mail: chc@hsph.harvard.edu
Web site: www.hsph.harvard.edu/chc

Dedicated to promoting healthy aging and encouraging ongoing community involvement, this initiative reaches out to retiring baby boomers through a national media campaign to reshape cultural attitudes regarding the senior years, and to encourage baby boomers to volunteer time and skills to their communities. The campaign is an outgrowth of the initiative's report, *Reinventing Aging: Baby Boomers and Civic Engagement*, published in June 2004, which found that the imminent great wave of retirees would be stimulated to turn their talents and experience to volunteer work. This report can be accessed through the initiative's Web site.

Immortality Institute (ImmInst)
1022 Stark St., Wausau, WI   54403
e-mail: support@imminst.org
Web site: http://imminst.org

ImmInst is an online network dedicated to supporting the search for a "cure" to aging. Founded in 2002, the organization promotes advocacy and research geared toward countering the natural limits of the human life span. ImmInst maintains a community blog and online forum.

International Longevity Center USA (ILC-USA)
60 E. 86th St., New York, NY   10028
(212) 288-1468 • fax: (212) 288-3132
e-mail: info@ilcusa.org
Web site: www.ilcusa.org

Founded in 1990 by gerontologist Robert N. Butler, whose book, *Why Survive? Being Old in America*, won the 1976 Pulitzer Prize, the International Longevity Center was the first nonprofit, nonpartisan, international research and policy organization formed for the purpose of educating individuals and society on how to maximize the potential benefits of aging. ILC-USA, one of an international consortium of independent longevity centers, performs extensive global research and provides education on age-related issues—health, politics, prejudice, caregiving—and their interrelationships. Many of its publications on these topics can be purchased or downloaded through its Web site.

Methuselah Foundation
PO Box 1143, Lorton, VA   22079-1143
(202) 306-0989
e-mail: main@methuselahfoundation.org
Web site: www.Methuselahfoundation.org

The Methuselah Foundation is a nonprofit organization committed to research on permanent remedies for age-related disease and disability. The foundation funds the Methuselah Mouse Prize (Mprize)—a competitive research prize for significantly extending the healthy life span of lab animals—and the SENS Research project, which is preparing a detailed plan to systematize the repair and reversal of all known forms of age-related damage to the human body. Foundation chair Aubrey de Grey is the author of *Ending Aging*.

National Institute on Aging (NIA)
Building 31, Room 5C27, 31 Center Dr., MSC 2292
Bethesda, MD   20892
(301) 496-1752 • fax: (301) 496-1072
Web site: www.nia.nih.gov

NIA, a department of the U.S. National Institutes of Health, is the leading organization in federal aging research. Its goals include developing a greater scientific understanding of aging, and finding ways to extend the healthy, active years of life. Established in 1974, the institute provides a variety of free publications (many available online) on such topics as caregiving, Alzheimer's disease, and other age-related issues.

Positive Aging Resource Center (PARC)

Brigham & Women's Hospital, Boston, MA   02215
(617) 525-6122
e-mail: sue-levkoff@hms.harvard.edu
Web site: www.positiveaging.org

PARC, established in 2002 as part of the Targeted Capacity Expansion (TCE) initiative of the Substance Abuse and Mental Health Services Administration (SAMHSA) to improve the quality of mental health care for older adults, provides resources for elders and their caregivers, including health and social service professionals. Its mission is to "promote positive aging." The Web site provides links to various books and periodicals related to geriatric mental health care.

President's Council on Bioethics

1425 New York Ave. NW, Suite C100
Washington, DC   20005
(202) 296-4669
e-mail: info@bioethics.gov
Web site: www.bioethics.gov

The President's Council on Bioethics, created in 2001 and renewed every two years, advises the president on ethical issues related to advances in biomedical science and technology. Its topics-of-concern list includes Age-Retardation (Life Extension) and End-of-Life; reports and transcripts are accessible through the Web site.

White House Conference on Aging

4350 East-West Highway, Bethesda, MD   20814
(202) 357-3507
Web site: www.whcoa.gov

The White House Conference on Aging was first held in 1961. Its purpose is to develop recommendations for age-related research and public action, and it considers input from a wide variety of participants, foci, and interests. The *Final Report* can be downloaded at the Web site.

Bibliography of Books

W. Andrew Achenbaum — *Older Americans, Vital Communities: A Bold Vision for Societal Aging.* Baltimore: Johns Hopkins University Press, 2005.

Robert N. Butler — *The Longevity Revolution: The Benefits and Challenges of Living a Long Life.* New York: PublicAffairs, 2008.

Robert L. Clark and Olivia S. Mitchell — *Reinventing the Retirement Paradigm.* Oxford: Oxford University Press, 2005.

Margaret Cruikshank — *Learning to Be Old: Gender, Culture, and Aging.* Lanham, MD: Rowman & Littlefield, 2003.

Aubrey de Grey and Michael Rae — *Ending Aging: The Rejuvenation Breakthroughs that Could Reverse Human Aging in Our Lifetime.* New York: St. Martin's Press, 2007.

Ken Dychtwald, Tamara J. Erickson, and Robert Morison — *Workforce Crisis: How to Beat the Coming Shortage of Skills and Talent.* Boston: Harvard Business School Press, 2006.

Maddy Dychtwald — *Cycles: How We Will Live, Work, and Buy.* New York: Free Press, 2003.

Margaret Morganroth Gullette — *Aged by Culture.* Chicago: University of Chicago Press, 2004.

Stephen S. Hall — *Merchants of Immortality: Chasing the Dream of Human Life Extension.* Boston: Houghton Mifflin, 2003.

Ed Kashi and
Julie Winokur

Aging in America: The Years Ahead.
New York: PowerHouse, 2003.

Harold G. Koenig

Purpose and Power in Retirement:
New Opportunities for Meaning and
Significance. Radnor, PA: Templeton
Foundation, 2002.

Laurence J.
Kotlikoff and
Scott Burns

The Coming Generational Storm:
What You Need to Know About
America's Economic Future. Cam-
bridge, MA: MIT Press, 2004.

Ray Kurzweil and
Terry Grossman

Fantastic Voyage: Live Long Enough to
Live Forever. Emmaus, PA: Rodale,
2004.

Phillip Longman

The Empty Cradle: How Falling Birth-
rates Threaten World Prosperity and
What to Do About It. New York: Basic Books, 2004.

M. Joanna Mellor
and Helen Rehr,
eds.

Baby Boomers: Can My Eighties Be
Like My Fifties? New York: Springer,
2005.

Sherwin B.
Nuland

The Art of Aging: A Doctor's Prescrip-
tion for Well-Being. New York: Random House, 2007.

Steven A. Nyce
and Sylvester J.
Schieber

The Economic Implications of Aging
Societies: The Costs of Living Happily
Ever After. New York, NY: Cambridge
University Press, 2005.

S. Jay Olshansky,
Leonard Hayflick,
and Thomas T.
Perls, eds.

Anti-Aging Medicine: The Hype and
the Reality. Washington, DC: The
Gerontological Society of America,
2004.

Organisation for Economic Co-Operation and Development — *Live Longer, Work Longer.* Paris: OECD Publishing, 2006.

Robert Palmer — *Age Well! A Cleveland Clinic Guide.* Cleveland, OH: Cleveland Clinic Press, 2007.

John Robbins — *Healthy at 100: The Scientifically Proven Secrets of the World's Healthiest and Longest-Lived Peoples.* New York: Random House, 2006.

Nancy K. Schlossberg — *Retire Smart, Retire Happy: Finding Your True Path in Life.* Washington, DC: American Psychological Association, 2004.

James H. Schulz and Robert H. Binstock — *Aging Nation: The Economics and Politics of Growing Older in America.* Westport, CT: Praeger, 2006.

David Snowdon — *Aging with Grace: What the Nun Study Teaches Us About Leading Longer, Healthier and More Meaningful Lives.* New York: Bantam, 2001.

Andrew Weil — *Healthy Aging: A Lifelong Guide to Your Physical and Spiritual Well-Being.* New York: Alfred A. Knopf, 2005.

Michael D. West — *The Immortal Cell: One Scientist's Quest to Solve the Mystery of Human Aging.* New York: Doubleday, 2003.

Eugenie G.
Wheeler

The Time of Your Life: The Best of Genie Wheeler's Columns on Aging Issues. San Diego: Tracks, 2005.

Index